Questions and

MARKETING

Howard Dunton BA MSc DipMRS

Principal Lecturer in Marketing and
Head of the Management & Business Studies Group
at The Hatfield Polytechnic

Longman
London and New York

Longman Group Limited
Longman House, Burnt Mill, Harlow
Essex CM20 2JE, England
Associated companies throughout the world

**Published in the United States of America
by Longman Inc., New York**

First published 1985

British Library Cataloguing in Publication Data

Dunton, Howard
  Marketing – (Questions and answers)
  1. Marketing
  I. Title   II. Series
  658.8   HT. 5415

ISBN 0-582-41329-X

Printed in Hong Kong
by Wing Lee Printing Co Ltd

Contents

Introduction

The purpose of this book is to help students who are studying marketing either as a specialism or a subsidiary subject. Many students find marketing a somewhat elusive or even vague subject where there often seems to be little agreement about what constitutes 'the right answer'. Despite studying carefully and at length, students can still have difficulty in understanding what the questions 'are getting at', or what 'the examiner wants'. Such problems are aggravated by the trend for questions to require the application of knowledge, often from a diverse range of marketing topics, to the analysis and solution of problems.

Conventional marketing textbooks are not written in this way. Therefore, the student is left with the problem of making the leap from the descriptions in the books (which do not always appear to be in agreement anyway!) to solving the problems posed in the questions.

This book gives examples from a range of questions, including a case study, with answers that help students to understand the scope and requirements of questions and provide an indication of the standard of answer expected. Thus, the book gives students a means of assessing and improving their knowledge in preparation for examinations and in-course assessment.

Thanks to my wife Gill for her excellent typing and for not complaining all the time.

Acknowledgements

We are grateful to the following for permission to reproduce copyright material;

Harvard Business Review for exhibit from *Strategies for Diversification* by H. Igor Ansoff (Sep/Oct 1957) Copyright (c) 1957 by the President and Fellows of Harvard College, all rights reserved; Plenum Publishing Corpn. for a formula from *Human Relations* 16 (1963) pp. 233–240.

To
LESTER YOUNG

If I could write
As he could play

| Question 1 | The Nature of Marketing | Answer page 11 |

'The aim of Marketing is to make selling superfluous.' Discuss.

| Question 2 | Marketing in Different Types of Market | Answer page 15 |

To what extent is Marketing relevant to different types of market?

| Question 3 | Marketing in Non-profit Organisations | Answer page 18 |

In what ways is Marketing used by non-profit organisations?

| Question 4 | The Marketing Plan | Answer page 22 |

Explain the nature and significance of the financial elements of the marketing plan.

| Question 5 | Growth Strategies | Answer page 25 |

Show how a manufacturer of do-it-yourself (DIY) paint stripper, wallpaper paste and plaster filler should decide on growth strategies.

Question 6   **Forecasting Market**   Answer page 28
                             Potential

By what means can market potential be forecast and of what practical use is this knowledge?

Question 7   **The Product Manager System** Answer page 32

What are the strengths and weaknesses of the Product Manager type of organisation, and how might the system be improved?

Question 8   **Buyer Behaviour Theory**   Answer page 35

What is meant by buyer behaviour theory? In what ways can buyer behaviour theory be of use to marketing managers?

Question 9   **Attitude and Behaviour**   Answer page 39

Examine the usefulness of attitude in forecasting buyer behaviour in the beer market.

Question 10   **Lifestyle**   Answer page 42

In which markets and in what ways is lifestyle a useful variable for segmentation?

Question 11   Group Influence

Answer page 45

Explain the effect of group influence on buyer behaviour.

Question 12   Perception Theory in Advertising

Answer page 48

Consider the importance of perception theory in the design of advertisements.

Question 13   Diffusion of Innovations

Answer page 51

Examine the relevance of diffusion of innovations theory to marketing management.

Question 14   Market Segmentation

Answer page 55

What is the purpose of dividing markets into segments? Describe the likely ways in which the following markets might be segmented:
(a) Breakfast cereals
(b) Diesel engines.

Question 15   Socio-economic Grade

Answer page 58

Socio-economic grade should be of fundamental importance in market segmentation. To what extent is this so, and how accurate are the results?

Question 16   ACORN and SAGACITY   Answer page 61

What advantages are offered by the segmentation variables ACORN and SAGACITY?

Question 17   Market Research Design   Answer page 65

A manufacturer of convenience foods is considering the introduction of a range of infant foods to the UK market. Recommend a research plan.

Question 18   Problems in Sampling   Answer page 68

What are the problems for market researchers in obtaining and using samples for data collection, and what means are available to overcome these problems?

Question 19   Sampling Methods   Answer page 71

Explain the following sampling methods:
(a) Probability sample
(b) Cluster sample
(c) Quota sample
(d) Multiphase sample
(e) Disproportionate sample.

Question 20   **Questionnaires**   Answer page 74

What are the major sources of inaccuracy arising from the use of questionnaires to collect market research data from consumers and how can such inaccuracies be minimised?

Question 21   **Retail Audits and**   Answer page 77
                    Consumer Panels

Why should a toiletries manufacturer require both retail audit and consumer panel data?

Question 22   **Qualitative Research**   Answer page 81

Explain the nature and methods of qualitative research and how it differs from quantitative research.

Question 23   **Advertising Research**   Answer page 84

How could advertising research be used in developing the creative aspect of an advertising campaign for a brand of instant coffee?

Question 24   **Test Marketing**   Answer page 88

Outline a test market procedure for a new brand of bottled fruit juice.

Question 25   **Industrial Market Research**   Answer page 92

What is industrial market research, and how does it differ from consumer market research?

Question 26   **Brief descriptions of...**   Answer page 97

Write brief descriptions of:
(a) BARB
(b) JICNARS
(c) JICRAR
(d) Hall tests
(e) Placement tests
(f) Omnibus studies
(g) *Ad hoc* research
(h) Observation studies
(i) Clinical research.

Question 27   **Product Life Cycle**   Answer page 102

In what ways is it possible to modify the Product Life Cycle?

Question 28   **The New Product Development Process**   Answer page 105

What are the major stages in the process of New Product Development?

What is the role of organisational structure in the process of New Product Development?

Examine the nature and purpose of product planning.

Describe the advertising communication process, and examine possible barriers to communication and the means by which these barriers might be overcome.

Assess the usefulness of models of advertising effect in explaining how advertising works and as a basis for planning advertising.

How is an advertising campaign created?

Question 34   **Promotional Mix**   Answer page 127

What is the promotional mix, and how can a company decide
on the mix to be used?

Question 35   **Determining the Advertising**   Answer page 131
                    Budget

Describe and assess the methods that can be used by a national advertiser to decide the size of the annual advertising
budget.

Question 36   **Advertising Agencies**   Answer page 135

Describe the functions and organisation of a full-service advertising agency.

Question 37   **Media Planning**   Answer page 138

Show how to design a media plan for an advertising campaign
for a new frozen snack.

Question 38   **Sales Promotion**   Answer page 142

What is sales promotion? Show how 'below-the-line' activity
is integrated into the overall promotional campaign.

Question 39   Economic and Social   Answer page 146
             Implications of Advertising

Discuss the proposition that in many markets the high cost of advertising works against consumer interests by raising prices and creating barriers to entry.

Question 40   Pricing a New Product   Answer page 149

Suggest a procedure for pricing a new miniature flat-screen hand-held television.

Question 41   Price as an Index of Quality   Answer page 153

What is the relevance to marketing management of consumers' use of price as an index of quality?

Question 42   Channel Development   Answer page 157

What are the factors that have led to the growth of superstores, and to what extent is the superstore concept likely to be applied to non-food retailing?

Question 43   Physical Distribution   Answer page 161
             Management

'Decisions about any single element in the physical distribution system should not be taken in isolation; it is the total cost of the system that is important.' Discuss.

Question 44	Sales Force Size and Structure	Answer page 165

By what methods could a national food company decide the size and structure of its sales force?

Question 45	Payment Methods for Salesmen	Answer page 170

How far is it possible to justify the existence of so many methods of paying salesmen?

Question 46	Industrial and Organisational Buying	Answer page 174

Examine the differences between industrial and consumer markets, and the implications of these differences for marketing management.

Question 47	Standardisation in International Marketing	Answer page 178

How can a company selling in more than one national market reconcile the conflicting objectives of 'tailoring' its marketing to meet the needs of each market with the achievement of savings possible through adopting standardisation in all markets?

A medium-sized British toy manufacturer wishes to begin marketing abroad. What procedure should the company follow?

Does the continued existence of consumerism indicate a continued absence of the marketing concept?

To what extent is consumer protection a major issue for marketing management in Britain?

Answer 1   The Nature of Marketing   Question page 1

1. Introduction

Marketing is the management process by which companies identify, anticipate and satisfy consumer needs profitably. A widely used definition is that of Kotler:

> 'Marketing is human activity directed as satisfying needs and wants through exchange processes.'

Marketing, or at least some of its techniques, is used in non-profit contexts, such as by the Army to attract recruits, and by the Ministry of Transport to dissuade car drivers from drinking alcohol. However, such applications are not relevant here.[1]

The profit-seeking company can be described as a set of variables over which management has considerable control. These variables are: production capabilities, financial resources, personnel, research and development and marketing. Surrounding the company is another set of variables over which the company has very little control: competition, supplies, economic, legal and social conditions, technological development, channels of distribution and consumers. This concept of 'controllable' company variables and 'uncontrollable' external variables is a generalisation commonly accepted in marketing textbooks. Nevertheless it should be noted that there is likely to be conflict within the organisation; for example industrial disputes, which cannot be completely controlled. Externally, however, despite the 1960s claims of J. K. Galbraith in *The New Industrial State,* the recession of the 1980s has shown that companies are not able to control their environment.

Figure 1 indicates marketing's role as the intervening factor seeking to match company variables or resources with external variables or opportunities.

Fig. 1

1. See answer to question 3 for more elaboration.

2. The Marketing Mix

The outcome of this matching process is the Marketing Mix (or Mixes). The Marketing Mix or '4 Ps' consists of the variables: Product, Price Promotion and Place (or distribution).

(a) *Product*: Design, quality, performance, style, packaging, guarantees, service.

(b) *Price*: Retail price, payment arrangements, credit and trade discount.

(c) *Promotion*: Advertising on television, radio, in the press and other media, sales promotion and personal selling.

(d) *Place*: Channels used and coverage, levels of stock carried.

The composition of the Mix is decided by marketing management on the basis of market research into the external variables, particularly consumers.

3. The Marketing Concept

The philosophy that firms exist primarily to satisfy consumer needs and wants is not always easily accepted, as the other business functions – Production, Personnel and Finance – understandably consider that they are as important, at least, as marketing. The fact is, however, that companies and the departments within companies achieve their objectives most effectively by recognising that their prosperity is dependent on meeting consumer needs.

Within the company, marketing can be seen as the function of organising the company's resources and activities around the needs and wants of consumers. This process is termed the *Marketing Concept* or being *consumer-oriented* and can be contrasted with the *Product Concept* or being *sales-oriented*, focussing not on the consumer but on the company and its products.

The Marketing Concept requires that the company's objective is to ascertain what consumers want and then set about making it; thus marketing decisions precede investment decisions. The Product Concept uses the idea that the sales volumes needed to sustain production efficiency can be achieved only by concerted heavyweight promotional and selling effort. Thus a declining product, overtaken by changes in consumer taste or technology, or a new product that has failed to achieve market acceptance, will receive massive promotion and selling in an attempt to create sales.

It might appear that, with every company being consumer-oriented, the result would be identical Marketing Mixes; for example, all toothpastes with the same taste, colour, packaging, price and advertising, and all cars of the same shape, price and performance, and so on.

The reason that this does not occur is that companies seek to give their Marketing Mixes *Differential Advantage*, i.e. make them not only attractive to consumers, but also distinctive from the Mixes offered by the competition. Moreover, these different Mixes are often targeted at different *Market Segments*. Crest is produced for those consumers chiefly seeking to reduce cavities, whilst Ultrabrite is aimed at the more socially-conscious.

4. The Importance of Selling

It might be concluded from the above that, by adopting the Marketing Concept to produce a Marketing Mix that is completely consumer-oriented and differentiated from the competition, sales resistance and therefore the need for selling would be eliminated.

However, it has been pointed out that selling, in the forms of salesmen, advertising and sales promotion, is a constituent of the Marketing Mix. Even for a product that fulfills a long-felt consumer need, i.e. is 'just what the consumer always wanted', for example a car that does 80 miles per gallon, it is necessary to advertise to inform consumers about the product's existence and performance. For products that are consumer-oriented but not functionally differentiated from the competition (for example, a shampoo) it is necessary to use advertising and selling to persuade consumers to buy the product – in fact to create the differential advantage.

Use of the Promotion element of the Marketing Mix applies to all types of market. In groceries, toiletries and alcoholic drink, for example, very intensive selling efforts are made to consumers through advertising and to retailers through salesmen. For consumer durables, such as washing machines and cars, both advertising and personal selling are used. And for industrial products, such as microcomputers and machine tools, salesmen are a major part of the Marketing Mix.

Promotion and selling remain important because it is

necessary to communicate with consumers and because companies have competitors. Therefore, sales and profit are dependent not only on Product, Price and Place, but also on energetic and skilful selling and promotion.

5. Conclusion

It can be argued that the aim of marketing should be to know and understand consumers so well that products and services offered are bought so eagerly that selling is unnecessary – i.e., the product should sell itself. However, because of competition, consumer unawareness and inertia, it is necessary to complement the other three mix variables with selling and promotion. If further proof is needed, consider that Japanese companies, for all their leadership in product design with low prices, are heavy users of the Promotion variable of the Marketing Mix.

Answer 2 **Marketing in Different Types of Market** Question page 1

---

1. Introduction

Marketing is the management process by which companies identify, anticipate and satisfy consumer needs profitably. The Marketing Concept requires that the company is organised around the objective of achieving differential advantage – the development and implementation of Marketing Mixes that are profitable by being attractive to consumers and distinctive from those of the competition.

As all markets necessarily have consumers and competitors, marketing is always relevant, in order to decide the nature of products to make, prices to charge, and promotion and distribution to employ. In marketing terms even so-called monopolies such as British Rail have competitors, as consumers can select between travel by rail, road, sea and air. Marketing, is applicable to markets as diverse as detergents and fork-lift trucks, but with significant variation in its role and importance in relation to the other business functions: production, personnel/industrial relations, finance and research and development.

2. Types of Market

First, it is necessary to identify the various types of market, and they can be classified as follows.

(a) *Consumer*: Where purchase is for consumption, either immediate or delayed.

(b) *Industrial*: Where purchase is for resale, reprocessing or to facilitate manufacture.

(c) *Service*: Where purchase is of intangibles.

(d) *International*: Where purchasers are located in more than one country.

3. Consumer Markets

These can be subdivided into *f.m.c.g.* (fast moving consumer goods) such as toothpaste, shampoos and breakfast cereals; and *consumer durables*, such as washing machines and cars. In many f.m.c.g. markets there is little or no functional or objective difference between competing products. There is no doubt that fluoride toothpaste is different from toothpastes without fluoride, and that anti-dandruff shampoo is more effective at curing this problem than other shampoos. However, despite the advertising claims, there is probably very little performance difference between different brands of anti-dandruff shampoos, fluoride toothpastes, concentrated washing-up liquids, low-lather washing powders, and so on. Moreover, the manufacturing technology of such products offers little opportunity for the production side of the business to provide innovations or cost reductions that are significant to consumers. For example, the only real product improvements in detergents have been low-lathering powders (for automatic washing machines) and enzyme powders.

Similarly, as the production processes of competitors are relatively simple and very similar, often with very limited opportunities for economies of scale, one firm cannot offer lower prices except by reducing unit profit. And in any case, price elasticity of demand is likely to be low, so that a very large price reduction would be necessary to produce a significant increase in sales. However, such an effective price reduction would lead to retaliation by competitors and possibly a price war.

In such markets, marketing's role is of great importance not just in developing new products and identifying consumer needs and wants, but also in creating differential advantage by branding, packaging and advertising.

A product such as Martini depends heavily on quite brilliant marketing for its success. Although the product is of good and consistent quality with a taste that has been developed to be pleasing to many customers, it was marketing that uncovered the demand for this type of vermouth drink. Further, it is marketing that has developed and maintained the product's smart and attractive image associated with young people and glamorous lifestyles. It is unlikely that technology could improve Martini's success, but without marketing it would be unknown.

Consumer durable markets also require the investigation and satisfaction of consumer needs and wants, and the creation of brand image.

For example, a company making washing machines must ascertain the sorts of wash and other functions required by users. It is also necessary to decide the most suitable market target and use advertising, promotion, distribution and pricing necessary to establish the brand with dealers and with consumers. However, because of the complexity of the manufacturing technology involved, there also exists scope for developing differential advantage through objective product features.

For example, if market research indicates that clothes drying is a major problem to buyers, it might be possible, through technology, to develop a faster spin speed or in-built dryer. Hence, differential advantage is achieved by a combination of marketing, production and research and development.

4. Industrial Markets

Again, the identification and satisfaction of buyer needs and wants is required – it is necessary to discover what sort of lathe, word processor or aeroplane is or will be in demand. But, industrial buyers are seeking and are able to discern objective features such as price, performance and delivery, and are unlikely to respond to sophisticated or intense advertising and branding. While it is necessary to research industrial markets so that products meet buyers' needs, it is the other business functions, production and research and development, that are most likely to produce the differential advantage.

5. Service Markets

These can be classified as subdivisions of industrial and consumer markets, so marketing has the relevance associated with these markets. In a *consumer* service market, such as retailing, marketing is used as extensively as in consumer product markets. The food retailers that have been most successful are those that have responded to consumer demand for wide range, low price and convenience shopping, by developing the very large 'superstores' with adjacent car-parking.

In *industrial* service markets, for example computer software, the successful companies are those that have used marketing to discover buyer needs, but also have had the technology to meet these needs quickly and at low cost.

6. International Marketing

In essence, this is the same as consumer or industrial marketing across national boundaries, so again the relevance of Marketing depends on whether the market is consumer or industrial.

7. Conclusion

By definition, marketing is relevant to all types of market. It is always necessary to identify and analyse the market – the consumers, competitors and the environmental factors that determine demand and profitable opportunities. However, marketing's role, relative to the other business functions, varies between markets.

This is not the same as simply saying that there is much more advertising, packaging and market research activity for consumer products than for industrial products. The essential principle is the need to analyse the contributions that the various business functions can make to the company's objective of making profits by identifying and satisfying buyers.

Answer 3	Marketing in Non-profit Organisations	Question page 1

---

1. Marketing in Profit and Non-profit Organisations

Traditionally, marketing is defined in terms of profit-seeking organisations operating within markets. Such definitions refer to marketing's role in producing revenue and profits for the organisation by identifying and satisfying consumer demand through exchange processes.

The Marketing Concept requires that the company is organised around the objective of achieving differential advantage – the development and implementation of Marketing Mixes that are profitable by being attractive to consumers and distinctive from those of competitors.

This consideration of marketing as being principally concerned with profit, competition and consumer demand does not appear, at first sight, to be compatible with non-profit applications.

The argument for the application of marketing to non-profit organisations and objectives is based on the proposition that they are confronted by problems which would be analysed as marketing problems if found in the profit sector. Just like any other business trying to manage its relationships and exchanges, the non-profit organisation has a marketing mix and seeks to understand and respond to its demand and environment.

2. Financial Non-profit Applications of Marketing

First, it should be noted that the term 'non-profit' does not necessarily imply 'non-financial', and many non-profit applications of marketing involve money transactions. For example, charities such as Oxfam have complete marketing operations and organise the manufacture and distribution of products.

In other cases, while there is no profit, revenue is sought to enable the organisation to continue to exist. For example, marketing is used by museums and galleries to increase the number of visitors by presenting and promoting attractive exhibitions. Similarly, opera and theatre companies use marketing in the selection and promotion of their productions. Many cultural organisations have used the marketing technique of sponsorship to obtain funds.

At a more localised level, social organisations, such as tennis and social clubs, use advertising to enrol new members.

3. Social Marketing

Whereas the objective of profit-marketing is, in essence, to make consumers part with money, the objective of Social Marketing is to increase the acceptability of a social idea, cause or practice. A controversial example is that of political candidates and parties seeking election and support.

However, the most widespread application is by governments: public health campaigns to reduce smoking and obesity; environmental campaigns to conserve resources and reduce litter; road-safety campaigns, to reduce drink-driving, to increase considerate and careful driving and child-safety.

Such campaigns have used market research both to identify the segments indulging most in the behaviour that it is sought to alter and to indicate the types of appeal most likely to be effective. These campaigns have used much the same techniques and referred to the same values as campaigns for products.

Anti-smoking advertisements have been targeted at young people of both sexes and have associated smoking with social ostracism; advertisements to discourage drink-driving, targeted at young males, have linked drunken driving not simply with financial penalties and imprisonment, but also with the foolishness and inconvenience of losing the driving licence, and guilt about injuring friends.

Anti-litter campaigns have been targeted at children, and used authority – figures relevant to this segment, such as footballers and pop stars.

4. Social Marketing and Profit Marketing

The extent to which non-profit marketing is the same as profit marketing depends on whether it uses the Marketing Concept or merely uses marketing techniques.

Simply using market research to define the market target and then spending large sums on promotion can be no more than a sales-oriented attempt to sell a product or idea regardless of whether it is wanted by consumers.

By following the Marketing Concept, an organisation would need to replace a product for which there is no demand. With social marketing however, this might not be possible, as the idea or cause is often predetermined and not susceptible to adaptation.

For example, market research might show that a museum is, in Levitt terms, in the wrong business and that it should transfer its resources and activities to more fashionable markets, such as discos or fast foods. While the museum management are unlikely to welcome such market-oriented solutions, they might consider the redesign and popularising of exhibits, the introduction of audio-visual guides and extension of opening times.

Similarly, a political party might make electorate-oriented alterations to its policies in order to maintain or increase support. In the USA, soccer has been marketed by modifications to the game rules and by consumer-oriented presentation and ground facilities. In the UK the marketing of soccer has been restricted to product-oriented advertising with no attention to the fundamental causes of consumer dissatisfaction.

Social marketing such as anti-smoking also appears product-oriented. However, in these cases marketing is used to identify and meet consumer preferences. Thus, it is not the negative aspects of not smoking that are emphasised but the positive health, financial and social advantages.

5. Conclusion

Some non-profit organisations regard marketing as a promotion function – a means of increasing or maintaining their current activities. Often, marketing can assist by promoting these activities or by developing a previously under-utilised aspect of the organisation's resources. For example, the finances of some colleges have been improved by renting the teaching and living accommodation for conferences and summer schools when not in use by the college.

Although apparently cynical, and definitely unfortunate, it is valid to ask whether as 'products' anti-smoking, museums or soccer have the characteristics to provide satisfaction to sufficient consumers to be profitable. If not, there are two marketing solutions.

First, modify these 'products' so that they do meet consumer needs and wants. Second, if this solution is not successful or possible, the products can be discontinued and the organisation's resources transferred to other products. In many cases non-profit organisations are unable or unwilling to take the fundamental marketing step of this second solution, and instead apply the marketing technique of promotion in what is no more than a product-oriented exercise.

1. Introduction and Definition

Planning is deciding now what to do later. The planning process consists of analysing the present situation, determining objectives and designing the tactics and strategies necessary to achieve these objectives. Within the company, planning can be categorised in terms of *time* and *scope*:

Time – *short-range planning*, covering a period of one year or less;

– *long-range planning*, covering periods of 3, 5, 10, or even 25 years.

Scope – *corporate planning*, covering the direction of the entire company, and involving all company functions;

– *functional or departmental planning*, covering the goals and strategies of one function, for example marketing.

Planning, particularly short-range, has three basic approaches. *Top-down* planning, in which goals and plans are set by top management for all lower levels. The opposite is *bottom-up*, where the various departments prepare their own plans and goals based on what they think they can achieve and send them to top management for approval. The most satisfactory approach, however, is *goals down – plans up*, whereby top management sets corporate goals and departments develop plans to achieve these goals.

The advantages that derive from planning are generally agreed to be:

(a) the encouragement of systematic thinking ahead by management
(b) better co-ordination of company efforts
(c) the development of performance standards for control
(d) better preparedness for sudden and unforeseen developments
(e) increased participation, commitment and co-operation on the part of executives.

2. Financial Elements of the Marketing Plan

Profits are required for the company to pay for its operations and to provide funds for development and growth, and it is essential that the cost and revenue data are comprehensive and realistic.

Comprehensiveness

Many companies have had financial problems arising from inadequate analysis of costs. Marketing costs include not only direct labour and materials, but also marketing expenditure on advertising, distribution and so on, and contributions to overheads such as heating, rates, computer etc.

Realism

The cost and revenue data in the plan are predictions of the future and, therefore, are subject to change. The forecast is based on expectations of the behaviour of influencing variables such as consumer responsiveness to the company's marketing expenditures, the level of competitive activity and the disposable income of the target group. Clearly, it is not possible to predict the timing and success of product launches by competitors. It is even less possible to predict the nature and effect of the climate, and brewers have found that the biggest single influence on sales is the weather.

This uncertainty does not mean that planning is a pointless exercise, but that it must take the uncertainty into account and incorporate upper and lower limits – 'optimistic' and 'pessimistic' forecasts – rather than a single figure.

3. Financial Elements of the Marketing Plan – Costs, Revenue and Profit

Marketing planning takes into account that different levels of expenditure produce different levels of sales and profit. While future figures are difficult to predict, a highly plausible outcome is shown in Fig. 2.

The rationale for Fig. 2 is as follows.

Sales response is low at small low levels as there is insufficient advertising and promotion to create more than minimal brand awareness. Larger budgets become more effective, but very large budgets cause only slight sales increase, as the target market is already very familiar with the brand.

Profits represent the sums remaining after marketing, production and other expenditures are deducted from sales revenue.

The problem is to define the effective band of expenditure. While it is never possible to know this in precise terms, the

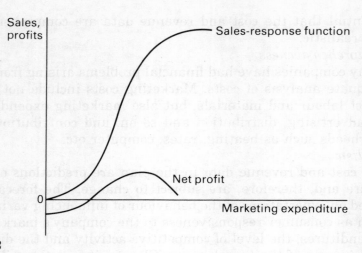

Fig. 2

'thresholds' of the bands are what advertising and marketing men refer to when talking about the 'support' required by brands. For a nationally marketed f.m.c.g. (fast moving consumer good) such as a shampoo or countline, the lower threshold is often well over £1 million. This figure varies between products and markets, but good approximations can be arrived at by experienced interpretation of the data available.

A further financial complication that the Marketing Plan must address is that decisions must be made not only on the level of marketing expenditure, but also on how this expenditure is allocated between and within each Mix variable. For example, a budget of £1 million could be used 60% for advertising, 20% for sales promotion and 20% for salesmen; or 80% for advertising, 20% for salesmen and nothing for sales promotion, and so on *ad infinitum*. Add to this that for each of these promotional combinations there is a choice of price levels, product quality and design and distribution expenditure, and the infinite range of financial marketing mixes is apparent.

4. Conclusion
Planning is essential to all human activity, especially where as with marketing, many factors are involved. Quantifying the behaviour and effect of marketing and environmental variables is complex and in most cases cannot be accomplished with great accuracy. However, as the achievement of market

24

ing objectives is assessed in financial terms it is essential that the Marketing Plan is also expressed in financial terms.

The solution to the need to quantify in an area that does not lend itself to quantification is to simplify. Thus, although it is necessary to be aware of all the relevant variables and influences, only the most operative should be included in the calculation, which in turn should recognise the impossibility of complete accuracy. Realistically broad forecasts should be made with all the assumptions made explicit. An estimate for beer sales that shows possible variations of up to 30% either way gives brewers the option of installing flexible capacity and is much more useful than an estimate that seeks accuracy that is not possible.

Answer 5   **Growth Strategies**   Question page 1

---

1. Introduction – the Theory of Growth Strategies
Most companies have growth of sales and profits as a major goal, because history shows that if companies do not grow, they do not stand still either – they shrink. The problem, then, is to decide the areas and directions in which the company should seek to develop and grow. The range of these choices is indicated in Ansoff's 'Product/Market Opportunity' matrix.[1] This essay will first explain the nature of these strategies and secondly consider them in the context of the DIY company.

(a) *Market Penetration*: The company seeks to expand sales of present products in its present markets by increasing fre-

		Market	
		Existing	New
Existing	**Product**	Market penetration	Market development
New		Product development	Diversification

Fig. 3

1. H. Igor Ansoff, 'Strategies for diversification', *Havard Business Review*, Sept./Oct. 1957, 113–24

25

quency and amount of use or by attracting new customers or both.

(b) *Market Development*: The company seeks sales for its present products in new markets.

(c) *Product Development*: The company develops new or modified products for sales in its present markets.

(d) *Diversification*: The company enters new markets with new products.

(e) *Integration*: The company obtains ownership or control of other parts of its manufacturing or marketing cycle.

2. Growth Strategies for a DIY Company

The DIY company's choice of growth strategy will be influenced by two sets of factors.

(a) Its own resources: finance, production, personnel and technological and marketing expertise.

(b) The estimated demand and competition in various markets.

The process of analysing these factors is often described as SWOT – the analysis of Strengths, Weaknesses, Opportunities and Threats.

Market penetration is a useful strategy if research shows that current DIY activity can be increased. For example, international or regional comparisons might indicate that in some areas decoration is infrequent. If, by promotion, this frequency can be increased, so that DIY decorating is done say, every three years instead of every five, sales of DIY products will rise. Alternatively, it might be possible to increase sales by increasing market share – attracting customers from competitors – by promotion, extended distribution or price competition. Sales could also be increased by converting non-users into do-it-yourselfers by emphasising the money to be saved, the high standard of finish possible and that no special skills are required.

If present markets are saturated, i.e. there is heavy and very effective competition, and all possible DIY users are decorating frequently, the company should consider *Market Development* – the expansion of its existing products into new markets. The company could enter export markets; attempt to attract women users by showing DIY as an acceptable female activity; seek new applications for its products, such as promoting the wallpaper adhesive as an all-purpose paper glue, or the filler for use on brickwork as well as plaster; or produce large pack sizes for trade use.

If demand for the company's existing products in *all* markets is saturated, it is necessary to seek growth by *Product Development*. This can take two forms. First, improvements and modifications to existing products, such as producing new colours and textures of filler; a paint stripper that works faster; or a filler that comes ready mixed, or in a resealable container. A second form of product development is to extend the product range by adding related DIY products such as varnish, a filler for motor vehicle body repairs or an adhesive for glass-fibre bonding.

If saturation has been reached for all the company's products and possible variations in all markets, the company could *Diversify* into new products for new markets. Whilst the scope here is unlimited, most companies choose to diversify on themes of current technology or current markets. The DIY company's chemical technology might be the basis for a range of cleaning products for ovens, machinery and similar heavy-duty uses. Alternatively, its existing market knowledge could provide the basis for an electric paint-stripper or ranges of DIY double glazing or shelving.

It is not necessary for diversification to have *any* link with the company's current operations. The company could move beyond chemicals and DIY to lauch new ranges of cakes or motorcycles, either by developing these products in-house or by acquiring companies already established in these technologies or markets. Whilst this form of 'conglomerate' diversification was popular in the 1970s, it is now regarded as the highest risk route to growth and would be a sensible strategy for the company only if all of the following criteria were fulfilled.

(a) All areas related to the company's current activities are static or declining, e.g. tobacco.

(b) The new areas afford particularly high growth potential, e.g. microcomputers.

(c) The company has large amounts of cash to invest, e.g. cigarette companies.

Lastly, growth can come from *Integration* with other parts of the company's manufacturing or marketing cycle. Integration can be *backwards* by obtaining ownership or control of supply systems and could involve the company in taking over raw material processors or packaging suppliers. This could require very high investment in companies to which the DIY company might represent a very small percentage of turnover. In addition, the DIY company would be entering an area of which it had very little knowledge and which would seriously restrict its flexibility.

Horizontal integration is growth by merger with or acquisition of competitors, in this case companies such as Polycell, Solvite and Marley. This strategy is attractive if there are significant economies to be gained from operating on a larger scale than the company can achieve on its own or if the company feels that at its present size there is a danger of being taken over on disadvantageous terms.

Forward integration involves obtaining ownership or control of distributive systems and would move the company into retailing. Again, this requires very high investment in an area where it probably has very little experience and which again reduces its flexibility by tying up capital. Moreover, ownership of some retailers can affect sales through others who might be resentful of the manufacturer's entry to their own market.

3. Conclusion

Growth is vital to the long-term survival of companies and can be achieved by a variety of strategies. As demand for DIY products is probably still expansible, the most logical strategies for the company are likely to be the penetration of new markets, the development of existing markets and the development of new products for these markets.

Answer 6   **Forecasting Market Potential**   Question page 2

1. Introduction and Definition

Market potential can be defined as the maximum level of purchases of a specific product or service by a specific customer group over a given time period with maximal level of marketing activity. An example is the amount of instant granule coffee (as opposed to powder or ground) purchased by households (as opposed to caterers and industrial users) in 1984, assuming that all brands were fully promoted.

Market potential can be compared with *Market Forecast* which is the level of sales *expected* to follow from an *expected* level of marketing activity. *The Company Sales Forecast* reflects the sales or market share that the company expects to achieve in a particular market. All these figures, but especially market potential, should be estimated for the short term (1 year) and the long term (around 5 years) to assist the company in its marketing, production and corporate plans.

2. Methods of Forecasting Market Potential

Some methods are *statistically based* using historical data. The simplest of these methods is *trend extension*, or *time series analysis*, which extends and 'smoothes' past sales patterns into the future, as in Fig. 4.

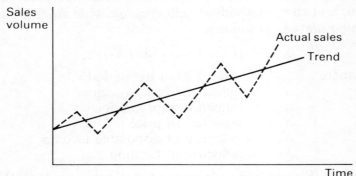

Fig. 4

This method can give an accurate forecast provided that the market is not volatile nor highly affected by external factors; for example, ice-cream sales are related less to past sales than to present weather conditions. There is also a danger that simple trend extension will miss turning points in the market, as shown in Fig. 5; the down-turn in sales might well indicate a fundamental change such as in the market for lever watches following the arrival of quartz.

More complex statistical methods seek to relate sales to other variables, such as income, prices, and promotion levels. These methods rely on being able to forecast these *independent variables* and, from these forecasts, derive the *dependent vari-*

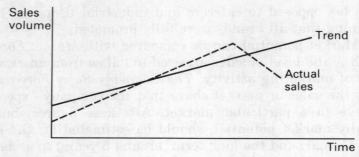

Fig. 5

able of demand for the product in question. For example, wine sales are related to variables such as social trends in leisure and entertaining, marketing expenditures on the product, economic factors, such as price, disposable income of the traget group and taxation on various alcoholic drinks. In a correlation model, the future performance of these variables is estimated, and their individual influence on wine sales weighted and aggregated, as follows:

$$S_t = f(X_1, X_2, X_3, X_4, X_5)$$

where: S_t = total sales in the period t
X_1 = influence of social factors
X_2 = influence of promotion
X_3 = influence of price
X_4 = influence of disposable income
X_5 = influence of taxation

With this method, it is necessary to estimate both the behaviour of the independent variables and their influence on sales. For this reason the method is criticised on the grounds that its only achievement is to change the problem of forecasting sales into the problem of forecasting other variables.

A more arithmetical approach is the *market build-up* method. Using this method, demand for wine would be determined by multiplying the estimated number of buyers by their estimated average purchase. When doing this, these consumers can be segmented geographically, or according to different levels of consumption.

3. Opinions
Rather than refer to past data to estimate the future, the com-

30

pany can seek opinions and attitudes of consumers, sales and marketing people, or consultants, towards the future. For example, a sample of consumers can be asked about their buying intentions – how much they expect to buy of a product during the coming six months, year or whatever. The method is most applicable to consumer durables, where consumers are asked about the probability of purchase during the period. In any case, the method depends on the extent to which consumers know their intentions and are willing to disclose them. For this reason, it is often the opinions of experts which are sought.

4. Test Market
The most accurate information and, for a new product, the only information, is obtainable from a Test Market. In this case the product and its proposed marketing campaign are launched for a test period in one or more areas that are representative of the total market. While this is obviously a method of measuring sales of one brand, rather than the market potential for *all* brands, the two figures might be very closely related in the case of a new product.

5. Usefulness to a Company of Market Potential Figure
Market potential derives mainly from macroeconomic and social factors and levels of industrial marketing activity, and is beyond the influence of individual companies, with two major exceptions. First, the market might be dominated by one very large seller, whose market share is so much larger than any other company in the market that its marketing expenditures constitute a sufficiently large proportion of total expenditure strongly to affect total consumption. Similarly, in a more fragmented market, sellers might combine to mount a marketing campaign aimed at increasing total sales in the market.

Normally however, market potential helps to determine the company's growth strategy by providing information on the levels of sales that can be achieved using various levels of marketing activity. For new or proposed products, market potential is a key indicator of which products should be developed, and for established products it acts as a bench-mark for planning and influences decisions on production schedules, promotion, price and distribution.

1. The Product Manager System

The most widely adopted solution to the organisational problems of marketing has been the Product or Brand Manager system which, it is conventionally felt, provides the flexibility and responsiveness required in a creative and dynamic business area in conditions of expanding company product lines and intense competition. The Product Manager system is a development of, and addition to, functional organisation, i.e. concentrating expertise among individuals or groups who are supervised by a departmental manager.

The Product Manager has been somewhat extravagantly described as a 'mini-managing director'. In theory, the system is the ultimate form of decentralisation and makes the Product Manager responsible for the development and implementation of marketing plans for his brand or brands. This responsibility can be broken down into six tasks:

1. Developing a long-range growth and competitive strategy for the product.
2. Preparing an annual marketing plan and sales forecast.
3. Working with advertising and merchandising agencies to develop copy, programmes and campaigns.
4. Stimulating interest in and support of the product among salesmen and distributors.
5. Gathering continuous intelligence on the product's performance, on customer and dealer attitudes and on new problems and opportunities.
6. Initiating product improvements to meet changing market needs.

2. Strengths and Weaknesses

The generally accepted advantages of the Product Manager system are:

1. Integrated attention for each brand rather than the fragmented treatment that would result from the various specialists working independently. The Product Manager can ensure a proper marketing mix.
2. Flexibility, as the Product Manager is able to respond quickly and autonomously to changes in the environment

without involving other people in meetings and discussions.

3. Adequate attention for all brands, even small ones, because of the individual Product Manager's competitive involvement.

4. Good training for subsequent senior management.

In reality this situation is difficult to create, mainly because the Product Manager system does not incorporate the fundamental management principle of parity of responsibility and authority. The Product Manager is not, in fact, a managing director, but rather a co-ordinator or ringmaster, whose success can depend greatly on his skill in working harmoniously with key people in the various functional departments. Further, he has the organisational problems of having to share a salesforce whose remotely controlled commission system might work against him, and of Sales, Advertising and Market Research Departments where managers are likely to be his senior. The Product Manager's archetypal youth is supposed to bring enthusiasm and energy, but can also mean that he lacks the necessary experience and training, especially in general management.

Another frustration of the Product Manager system ideal is the extent and variety of calls on his time. Anyone who has spent any time observing Product Managers will know that they are not exempted from the phenomenon that the trivial and immediate receives priority over reflection and strategy formation. Typically, the Product Manager is seen as an act of juggling Neilsen, TGI and AGB figures, calls on his time and budget from Market Research, Advertising and Sales, pack redesign, product modification, feedback and complaints from salesmen and customers, and numerous other problems associated with the Marketing Mix. Consequently, very little time is available for consideration or long-term planning.

At a more sociological level, the job tenure of Product Managers tends to be brief. Moving on within or outside the company, again reduces the likelihood of continuity or long-term planning from Product Managers to whom it might appear more personally profitable to seek jam today. And, the competition between Product Managers can lead to wasteful conflict rather than synergy. Lastly, by its very name, the Product Manager system commits the cardinal marketing sin of not being consumer-oriented.

3. Proposals for Improvement

The Market Manager system and its variations are attempts to overcome the disadvantages of the Product Manager system whilst maintaining its advantages. Where a company has an essentially homogeneous or at least closely related line of products which appeal to different segments of the market, the Market Manager approach may make more organisation sense, since it may put appropriate focus on each of the marketing opportunities. However, the Market Manager still has a high-level responsibility for getting a product to market without any direct line authority over the full range of activities necessary to get that job done. It is this similarity that makes almost everything that can be said about the problems of the Product Manager valid also for organising the Market Manager's job.

Nevertheless the Market Manager system does offer the advantages of market-orientation and has been adopted in some companies marketing products such as ice-cream, oil, paper and alcoholic drinks.

A development of the Market Manager system is to combine it with the Product Manager system. The Market Manager plans what company products should be sold and in what volume to his group of markets, aided in this process by the Product Managers who stress the suitability of their own products for each market. The Product Managers link the plans of the Market Managers with sales, promotion and manufacturing, and also provide detailed product knowledge.

Another way of meeting the problems of marketing organisation is 'federal' decentralisation, advocated in particular by Drucker, whereby divisions are established for products or product groups. As noted previously, this system becomes unworkable for products with small turnovers.

4. A More Realistic Product Manager System

It has been suggested that the Product Manager system can be improved by:

(a) Recognising the limitations of the Product Manager's role and responsibility by defining the job as 'proposer' rather than 'decider', and measuring his or her achievements in terms of extent of this authority.

(b) Forcing him or her to think in strategic terms by requiring planning to be done in those terms.
(c) Minimising or eliminating conflict with other departments by defining who is responsible for which decisions; and establishing a procedure for settling disagreements.

5. Conclusion

If it is accepted that at least in multi-product companies marketing organisation needs flexibility and responsiveness, the Product Manager system, possibly with some modification, does appear to offer the best solution. Obviously, the success of any organisational system is in the implementation but the suggestions do contain certain hopeful elements:

(a) They make explicit the problems associated with the system.
(b) They seek to compensate for these problems by redefining the Product Manager's job and clarifying his or her environment.
(c) They do not depart from principles of management that history has shown to be indispensable to successful organisation structures.

Answer 8   **Buyer Behaviour Theory**   Question page 2

1. Buyer Behaviour

Buyer behaviour can be defined as 'the acts and decisions of individuals and groups, leading to purchase of products and services'.

Two points about this definition should be noted. First, that buying can be done by *individuals*, for example a man buying a razor for his own use; and *groups*, such as a company buying a computer, or a family deciding on a vacation. Second, the use of the term 'buyer', rather than 'consumer', indicates that the two are not necessarily the same. For example a housewife buys food to be consumed by the entire family and clothes to be worn by her children or husband.

2. Buyer Behaviour Theory

Theory is concerned with providing a coherent study and systematic structure for a field of study. It involves: (a) postulating a number of key variables, e.g. market forces, such as advertising and price, or consumer characteristics, such as motives and attitudes; (b) specifying causal relationships among these variables, e.g. effect of advertising on attitudes; and (c) indicating the extent to which changes occur over time, either within the variables themselves, or in their inter-relationships.

While buyer behaviour has been examined in many ways, there is a major distinction between *stochastic* and *behavioural* models.

Stochastic models predict buyer behaviour by measuring probabilities based on records of past purchases. For example, a consumer who bought Ski yoghurt on six of the last ten purchasing occasions would be given a 0.6 probability of buying Ski yoghurt on the next occasion (although this figure can be weighted by the relative recency of the Ski purchases). By aggregating such examples and comparing with the population, forecasts of sales by brand can be estimated. Stochastic models, then, concentrate on what is purchased rather than on the underlying causal processes. However, the method gives no explanation of the *reasons* for purchase and is of little use in predicting how buyer behaviour responds to marketing activity such as advertising or sales promotion. Further, it can be applied only to frequently purchased products.

Behavioural models have been far more widely developed, if not more widely used in practice than stochastic models, and originate from the behavioural theories of economics, sociology and psychology. They derive from the fundamental proposition:

$$B = f(IE)$$

where: B = behaviour
I = variables *internal* to the consumer (attitudes, perception, motives, personality, lifestyle demography.
E = variables *external* to the consumer (group influence, class, culture, marketing)

Behavioural models demonstrate, by means of flow charts, how these variables interact and determine purchase. Typical examples of those of Howard, Nicosia and Engel, Blackwell and Kollat.

3. Usefulness of Buyer Behaviour Theory to Marketing Managers

Buyer behaviour is central to the understanding and practice of marketing. The Marketing Concept shows the need to organise the company around consumers and to design Marketing Mixes that will be attractive to consumers. All decisions on advertising, product design, price and distribution must be made in terms of the effect on buyer behaviour.

However, the application of buyer behaviour theory is confronted by the contradictory objectives of making the theory both sufficienty *comprehensive* to be valid and sufficiently *simple* to be understandable.

Comprehensiveness

A buyer behaviour theory must incorporate the range of variable combinations given by the multidimensional matrix of:

(a) different consumers
(b) acting differently according to
(c) different type of purchase
(d) different environmental stimuli;

i.e. the range from a housewife's repeat purchase of washing powder to the joint purchase of a machine for industrial use.

Simplicity

Attempts to simplify theories and models can omit or generalise information to the extent that the result is invalid.

It is not surprising, therefore, that buyer behaviour theory in the academic sense of the classic models of Howard, Nicosia and Engel, Kollat and Blackwell has not been widely adopted by managers. However, the theory has direct and indirect contributions to make in the following ways:

(a) by establishing the principle of the buyer behavioural process with several stages and constituent variables.
(b) by specifying a framework that can be adopted to various markets, allowing variables to be identified or made explicit and estimated, if not measured with any accuracy.

4. Application of Buyer Behaviour Theory to Marketing Practice

In order to apply theory directly to buyer behaviour it is necesary to *simplify*; not in the manner criticised above, but by controlled selection. To attempt to account for every phenomenon may lead to confusion. A primary function of a theory is to delimit the area being embraced – to clarify what aspects are being covered and what are not.

This delimiting can be done in two ways:

1. Concentrate on one variable, or set of variables considered to be the most relevant in general, or to a specific market. For example, attitudes are often taken as the most important influence on behaviour, and thus personality, motivation and perception are excluded as duplicative. The formation of attitudes by social influence and other external factors are considered irrelevant and confusing, at least in the creation of a model designed only for static description.

2. Derive a model for types of market or product, e.g. the 'low' and 'high' involvement model of Engel, Kollat and Blackwell, or the industrial buyer behaviour model of Sheth.

In fact, both these approaches are very similar, the difference being that the first starts from consumer behaviour and moves onto the product/market, whereas the second proceeds the opposite way.

5. Examples of Modelling in Practice

(a) The use of attitude-based models to segment markets in order to search for gaps that can be filled profitably. For example, a low-calorie beer with a full-strength masculine image; or a range of low-calorie spiced convenience meals.

(b) In an industrial market, a range of low-priced coaxial connectors was developed when research among users showed that low cost was more important than very high quality standards.

(c) The UK male shaving market was modelled to show the differing requirements and responses of various segments. For example, users of wet shaving are less motivated by convenience than users of electric shavers. Further, the buyers of electric shavers can be divided into gift buyers (usually women buying for men) and male own-use buyers. In each case, influences on purchase vary in importance.

6. Conclusion
As buyer behaviour is central to the understanding and practice of marketing, some method of prediction is extremely valuable. The logical route to achieve this is through the incorporation of the operative variables in a model, but this can be counter-productive unless some disciplined form of selection and limiting is employed.

Answer 9   **Attitude and Behaviour**   Question page 2

1. The Nature of Attitude
Allport's famous definition[1] of attitude as 'learned predispositions to respond to an object or class of objects in a consistently favourable or unfavourable way' suggests a link between attitude and buyer behaviour.

There are two major influences on the development of an individual's attitudes. First, his or her experience – in the case of beer, exposure to the advertising packaging and consumption of various brands. Second, the experience and the social influence of others, either individually or in groups, providing information about their own experience or social pressure to conform.

An individual's attitude towards a product (or, indeed any object) is determined by the attributes he believes the product to possess, weighted by the desirability to the individual of these attributes. For example, if an individual believes that a particular brand of beer is strong, and that strong beer is desirable, then this will contribute to a favourable attitude to this brand of beer. Another individual might also believe that the brand of beer is strong, but that strength is not desirable. In this case, the same attribute of strength will contribute to an unfavourable attitude to the brand.

1. Gordon W. Allport, 'Attitudes', in *Handbook of Social Psychology*, ed. C. A. Murchinson (Worcester, Mass.: Clark University Press, 1935), pp. 798–844

For most individuals and for most products, attitude involves a range of such attributes. In the case of beer, these might be strength, sportiness, masculinity and expensiveness. A brand's possession of these attributes, as perceived by the individual, plus the desirability to the individual of these attributes, can be measured by market research. Using these data, the individual's attitude towards the brand can be assessed, on the basis of various attitude models.

2. Attitude Models

The most celebrated of these is the *compensatory model* usually associated with Martin Fishbein.[2] This model postulates the consumer evaluating a brand in terms of its attributes and the desirability of those attributes, and then producing a sum. The model is expressed in the formula:

$$A_o = \sum_{i=1}^{n} B_i a_i$$

where: A_o = attitude towards the object
          B_i = the attributes that the consumer believes the object to possess
          a_i = the consumer's evaluation of these attributes
          n = the total number of attributes.

The application of this model in Fig. 6 indicates the manner in which the 'low' scores of some attributes can be *com-*

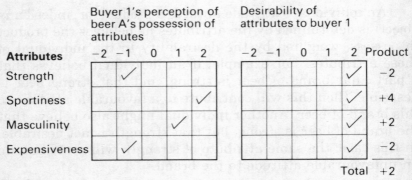

Fig. 6

2. Martin Fishbein, 'An investigation of the relationship between beliefs about an object and the attitude toward that object', *Human Relations* **16** (1963) 233–40.

pensated by 'high' scores of others. Figure 6 shows that Buyer 1 regards Brand A as fairly weak but also that he regards strength as desirable. Therefore, this is a minus for Brand A as far as he is concerned. As this minus is compensated by an equivalent plus on the attribute of sportiness, Brand A's overall score is +2.

If this process is repeated for competing beer brands, the buyer's purchasing can be forecast by the brand achieving the highest score.

For some products and buyers, other attitude models might offer more accurate representations of the relationship between attitude and behaviour.

Conjunctive model

Instead of compensating 'weak' attributes with 'strong' attributes, a buyer might require that *all* attributes reach certain minimum levels. For example, unless a brand of beer is masculine and sporty, above a certain strength and below a certain price, the buyer's attitude would be that it is unacceptable.

Disjunctive model

The buyer might reject the beer unless it reached specified levels on one or more key attributes, with the other attributes being of little importance. For example, the beer might be purchased provided that it is above a certain strength, and below a certain price, regardless of its scores for masculinity and sportiness.

Lexographic model

In this case, the buyer *ranks* the attributes of the various beers and the brand that scores highest on the most important attribute is the most favoured

3. Attitude and Behaviour

It should be emphasised that whilst the above four models are representations of different ways in which consumers judge brands, they are not consciously followed or selected by consumers.

Further, despite these developments in the analysis of attitudes, it has often been found that there is poor correlation between attitude, as expressed and measured and subsequent buying behaviour. There are five main reasons for this paradox.

First, attitude can be formed *after* purchase or use, so that a measured attitude can develop further after experience with the brand. For example, an individual might change from a neutral to a favourable attitude towards a beer after trying it on a few occasions.

Second, attitude might differ between the times of measurement and purchase because of a change in other factors. For example, market changes, such as a price increase or an advertising campaign; or a change in the weather, which might well influence a decision to buy beer.

Third, it should be noted that attitude is only one determinant of buyer behaviour, and inevitably omits or at best understates the influence of social factors.

Fourth, it might be impossible to discriminate between attitudes in some cases. For example, a buyer might consider that all brands of a beer are so similar that his attitude towards each brand is apparently identical.

Fifth, through inadequate research it is possible to overlook those attributes that are important or 'salient' in the buyer decision.

4. Conclusion

Attitude can be helpful in forecasting buyer behaviour, but it is essential to use the variable correctly, by referring to the model appropriate to the type of buying decision and by ensuring that the research data take account of the causes of discrepancy between attitude as measured and buying as observed.

Answer 10　　　　**Lifestyle**　　　　Question page 2

1. Definitions

Lifestyle is the individual's system of attitudes, beliefs, opinions and is a major influence on his/her patterns of living and spending. Application of the concept to marketing began in the early 1970s and it has proved of great value in understanding a wide range of buyer behaviour and in segmenting certain markets. The term *psychographics* is often used as a synonym for lifestyle, to demonstrate the contrast with *demographics*, but also as a description of the methods and techniques used in the measurement of lifestyle.

The theory of lifestyle is a development from that of personality which, despite repeated attempts, has not been successful in the explanation of consumer behaviour.

Lifestyle theory is based on the assumption that individuals seek to develop a 'persona' or 'front' with which to relate to the world. Although this lifestyle can change over time, it tends to be consistent internally and with the individual's behaviour.

2. Lifestyle and Marketing

Lifestyle is attractive to marketers for two basic reasons. First, it is a simple yet valid summary of the major variables used in buyer behaviour theory, i.e. attitudes, perception and social influence. Second, lifestyle influences an individual's purchasing, as he will tend to select those products and services which match or enhance his lifestyle.

For marketing's purpose, lifestyle can be analysed either generally or in specific, 'tailor-made' forms. A celebrated generalised lifestyle study segmented men into categories such as the 'Quiet family man', the 'Ethical highbrow' and the 'He-man'. Purchasing patterns would be expected to be closely related to these lifestyle types. The 'Quiet family man' might well be more likely to buy books, do-it-yourself home improvement products and insurance than the 'He-man' who is likely to be a major buyer of beer and sporting goods.

Greater accuracy and discrimination is possible using 'tailor-made' studies, carried out for particular markets or products. For example the 'Cosmopolitan', 'Traditional home-cook' and 'Health-conscious' among housewives in food markets.

3. Lifestyle Measurement

As mentioned above, lifestyle measurement is often referred to as psychographics and is achieved by recording an individuals agreement (or disagreement) with AIO (Activities, Interests, Opinions) statements, such as:

'I like to do all my own car maintenance.'
'I always watch Dallas on TV.'
'Buying things on credit is to be avoided.'

Reaction to up to fifty such statements might be measured in a lifestyle study, but it can be seen that agreement or disagreement with any *one* of these statements gives an indication of an individual's lifestyle.

4. Lifestyle and segmentation

For segmentation, lifestyle provides a dimension of information on a buyer that is simply not available from demographics. For example, traditional (and very useful) demographic segmentation might describe whisky drinkers as AB, male, aged 45 plus. While this segment might well account for the major part of whisky consumption, it inevitably excludes some buyers. More important, it does not discriminate between those AB males, 45 plus, who drink whisky and those who drink other spirits, wine, nothing, or who drink whisky in varying degrees of frequency or quantity.

Further, demographic segmentation merely *identifies* buyers and users and gives no indication of the reasons for purchase. The whisky drinker's demographic description can be amplified with the psychographic data that he is likely to be traditional and conservative in outlook with outgoing, active interests, whereas a gin drinker of the same demographics is likely to be modern and trendy with interests in the arts.

Such information can assist in marketing decision-making. First, products can be positioned in the market to match lifestyle segments that offer sales potential, either because they are not presently served or because of sheer size. Second, advertising can be designed to appeal to lifestyle segments, by use of appropriate settings, dialogue, actors, music and so on. Third, in some cases at least, it is possible to place advertising in media that will reach the lifestyle segment sought, and thus avoid the wastage of using more generalized media. For example, various women's magazines clearly appeal to different lifestyles, such as home/cooking-oriented and modern/independent.

Lifestyle is most useful in explaining markets which offer opportunities for buyers to express their lifestyles. These are often concerned with products that are conspicuous in use, such as alcoholic drink, cigarettes, clothing and some consumer durables, but can include more mundane items, such as food and household cleaners. For example, food that is (or sounds) foreign or modern will appeal to cosmopolitan, progressive lifestyles; high-fibre foods will appeal to those with healthy lifestyles; and self-shine floor polish will not appeal to housewives whose lifestyle is home-oriented and puritan.

In some markets demography remains the overriding variable in explaining buying. For example, the major buyers of baked beans and detergents can be described as female with young children. Even in markets such as this, lifestyle might be of use in discriminating between buyers of branded beans and those who buy private label.

5. Conclusion

Lifestyle is a key variable in segmenting many markets and can be of great assistance in decision making about product development and design and advertising. Although, in some cases, demography is the dominant variable, lifestyle can still be usefully applied to discriminate between certain classes of buyers.

Answer 11   **Group Influence**   Question page 3

1. Types of Group Influencing Buyer Behaviour

There are a number of types of groups that affect buyer behaviour. These are known as reference groups, as it is to the norms or standards of these groups that the individual *refers* when making a wide range of decisions, including buying decisions. It is important to note that although a reference group is one by which the individual evaluates himself and his behaviour, he does not have to be a member of that group. In general, reference groups affect an individuals behaviour in three ways. First, they expose him to new behaviour and lifestyles. Second, the norms of the group affect his own attitudes, values and behaviour, in his desire to conform, or 'fit in'. Third, the group has an informational role and provides guidance when assessing alternative purchases.

Reference groups can be classified as follows.

(a) *Membership groups*: Groups to which the individual belongs. These can be subdivided into *primary* groups, with which the individual has frequent 'face-to-face' contact, such as the family and close friends; and *secondary* groups, such as professional and political groups, where face-to-face contact is infrequent or even non-existent.

(b) *Aspirational groups*: Groups whose standards are perceived as favourable by the individual and which he aspires to join.

(c) *Dissociative groups*: The opposite of aspirational groups, whose norms are perceived by the individual as unfavourable and to be avoided.

2. The Family

Of all reference groups, it is undoubtedly the family which has the greatest effect on buying behaviour. The family's role in socialisation provides a long-term set of values, often affecting lifestyle, and is a major determinant of day-to-day purchasing. This powerful influence results from the family's unique group characteristics as an economic unit, with its own income and also as a consumption unit, whose purchasing directly affects all members.

The extent of the family's influence varies according to its lifecycle and values, and extends to all purchases which involve more than one member of the family, in terms either of *product use* or the *funds required for purchase*.

Product use: The purchase of consumer durable products will be affected by all family members involved in their use. For example, with the purchase of a car, husband, wife and children will have opinions on factors such as price, performance, ease of parking, space to carry toys and bicycles and so on. Similar considerations apply to the purchase of a television set or holidays. In all cases, the relative roles and importance of individual family members will vary.

The choice of frequently purchased products can also be influenced by the family because of shared use. For example, food, where the tastes and preferences of family members will greatly influence the housewife's buying.

Some products for individual use will also be affected by the norms of the family, if they are conspicuous in use. For example, clothing, particularly that of adolescent children.

Funds required for purchase: The purchase of an inconspicuous but high-cost product, used by only one member, will be subject to family influence because of the effect it has on the capability of the family to buy other products. An example of such a product is a set of golf clubs. The only purchases not influenced by the family, then, are those:

(a) where the choice affects only one member of the family in use
(b) which are of minimal cost
(c) which conform to the family's norms of behaviour.

3. Other Reference Groups

After the family, it is the other membership groups that are likely to have most effect on purchasing. This influence operates particularly on the purchase of products that are conspicuous in use, for example, clothing, cars, cigarettes and alcoholic drink, where the individual will tend to buy products and brands that are compatible with the norms of the various groups of which he is a member. For example, a member of a football club will drink beer of a certain brand, rather than Martini, at least when with his football club friends. Membership groups also influence the individual by giving advice on products, the purchase of which is associated with high risk due to technical complexity, high cost or the buyer's lack of knowledge.

The influence on purchasing of aspiration and dissociative groups is difficult to assess, but its importance appears to be great to many advertisers, to judge from campaigns which associate products with the lifestyles of desirable groups, such as the 'Martini People'.

4. Conflict Between Reference Groups

Conformity to the norms of one group might involve behaviour that is incompatible with those of another. For example, a husband's purchase of an estate car or hatchback to satisfy family requirements might be at odds with the norms of his workplace or leisure groups.

This conflict can be resolved by the buyer referring to his hierarchy of groups and conforming to the norms of the one he least wants to offend – probably the family. Alternatively he might compromise, by buying a GT version of the estate or hatchback, or he might postpone the decision.

5. Summary of the Importance of Group Influence on Marketing

Group influence is prevalent in many types of buying decision, and can be used to the advantage of marketing in two major ways. First, by showing in advertisements how products will meet with the approval of relevant groups, especially the family. Campaigns often emphasise a product's contribution to various roles within groups, especially that of mother within the family. Second, by the use of advertising and the development of products to reduce conflict within and between groups.

Answer 12   **Perception Theory in Advertising Design**   Question page 3

---

1. Definition

It has been estimated that an average person is exposed to over 1000 advertisements a day. And, advertising is only one of the stimuli in which that person is likely to be interested. In order to produce a coherent and meaningful picture from such potential confusion, the individual selects, organises and interprets the stimuli he receives through the five senses. This process is termed *perception*, and accounts for the fact that different people have different interpretations or perceptions of the same situation or event. What is actually perceived by the individual is a function of three sets of factors.

(a) *The characteristics of the object/situation/event*: For example, a large advertisement in black and white.

(b) *The physical characteristics of the individual*: Some people can read at greater distances than others, or understand more complex messages.

(c) *The individual's reference frames, or 'cognitive' map of the world.*

2. Reference Frames

Reference frames (also referred to by some writers as cognitive structures and evaluative criteria) represent summaries of an individual's beliefs, experiences, attitudes and feelings about objects or groups of objects. For example, he might have one reference frame that French wine is expensive, 'less fattening' and drunk by smart people with meals; and another that beer is inexpensive, fattening and drunk by ordinary people on its own.

These reference frames are a convenient and simple summary of numerous and complex attitudes towards these two drinks and provide a basis for making decisions about purchasing. The individual expects French wine and beer to conform or be *consonant* with his reference frames.

Information that is in conflict will cause *cognitive dissonance*, which is uncomfortable, in a similar way to physical discomfort. Provided that all information received by the individual is consonant with his appropriate reference frame, there is no problem. Indeed the individual will tend to seek out and pay attention to messages that are consonant with his reference frames. However, it is likely that some messages will be dissonant, for example, a brewing company advertising that its beer is not fattening and is suitable for consumption with meals.

The individual can deal with a dissonant message – one that is in disagreement with one (or more) of his reference frames – in two ways:

(a) He can change the reference frame, so that he now believes that beer is not fattening, and is suitable for consumption with meals.

(b) He can perceive the message in such a way as to remove the dissonance.

The strategy adopted by the individual depends primarily on the strength with which the reference frame is held; often a combination is used.

3. Perceptual Distortion.

The second strategy is termed perceptual distortion and occurs as follows:

(a) *Selective attention*: The individual seeks advertisements which are quickly recognisable as being consonant with his interests and beliefs, and pays little attention to others.

(b) *Selective perception*: The individual alters or rationalises dissonant information, so that it becomes consonant with his reference frame. In the beer example he might consider that the advertiser is biased or that the presenter is 'just saying that because he's paid to'.

(c) *Selective recall*: The individual remembers messages that are consonant and forgets those that are dissonant.

4. Perception and Advertising Design

As examined above, perception theory shows that unless an advertisement tells the consumer something he wants to hear, it will tell him nothing at all, as it will be perceptually distorted so that it is consonant with his reference frame.

Ideally advertisements should be designed so that they present the product in the most favourable way that is also consonant with the reference frames of the audience. The favourable aspects should be emphasised and the less favourable aspects omitted. Thus an advertisement for French wine in our example would draw attention to the product's smartness and skip over its expensiveness.

However, it is often necessary to use a message, the object of which is to persuade or to change reference frames that are unfavourable to the product. In such a case, the persuasive message runs into conflict with the pre-existing beliefs that it is seeking to change. In the beer example, attempts to overcome this can take one of three forms:

(a) Emphasising attributes of the product favourable to the targets' reference frame, for example, the beer's inexpensiveness.

(b) Downgrading the effect of the unfavourable (fattening) attribute, for example, 'What's wrong with being well-built? Who wants to be skin-and-bones?'

(c) Introducing new information, for example that some change in the recipe or brewing process now causes the beer to be less fattening.

5. Perception Theory and Subliminal Advertising

Subliminal advertising – the use of stimuli below the level of conscious perception – is banned in all major advertising countries. However, it is doubtful whether, even if legal, it would be greatly used, as it is a technique of great limitation and unpredictability rather than a powerful tool of brainwashing

6. Fear in Advertising

Extensive research has shown that 'high-fear' advertisements tend to be ineffective, due to selective attention – the audience is so frightened that it 'switches off'. In contrast, 'low-fear' or anxiety' advertisements, such are used for toothpaste, are effective provided that some reassurance is offered.

These advertisements do not say, 'Unless you use this product your teeth will fall out and you will have excruciating pain'. Rather, they say, 'There is a danger that you will need fillings/have yellow teeth/have bad breath. This danger can be avoided by regular use of this very pleasant product'.

7. Conclusion

Perception theory shows that consumers are most likely to be influenced by advertisements with which they are in agreement. Advertisements should be, and can be, designed within this constraint (as well as within the constraints of the law and other advertising regulations) whether the objective is to reinforce or to change behaviour.

Answer 13   **Diffusion of Innovations**   Question page 3

---

1. Definitions

The 'Diffusion of innovations' describes the process by which new ideas, beliefs, behaviour patterns and products are propagated and adopted among a given population. In this definition, *adoption* refers to consumers' progress from unawareness of the innovation, through interest, evaluation and trial to purchase and, in the case of quickly-consumed goods, repurchase.

The term *innovation* is more complex in terms of what constitutes an innovation, and to whom. A useful marketing definition is 'any product that has recently become available on the market'.

The 'newness' or extent of the innovation varies along a continuum. At one end are *continuous* or minor innovations, the adoption of which causes little or no disruption to the existing patterns of consumption; examples are a new pack design for a soap powder or an additional fragrance for a deodorant. The opposite are discontinuous innovations, the adoption of which necessitates a major change in consumption patterns, for example a microwave oven.

Between these two extremes are *dynamically discontinuous* innovations, which can be adopted by some modification of existing consumption patterns; examples are the electric toothbrush (still a toothbrush) and the pushbutton telephone (still a telephone).

2. The Diffusion Process

It is very rare that an innovation achieves simultaneous and immediate acceptance throughout a market. (The products that have probably come closest to this were the Beatles records of the 1960s which were Number 1 hits on their day of release). Indeed, the Product Life Cycle Concept[1] derives in major part from the fact that a new product is adopted (and discarded) at varying times by different consumers – see Fig. 7.

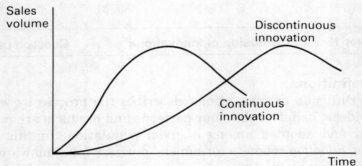

Fig. 7

Consumers have been analysed on the basis of the time required to adopt an innovation and segmented into the five 'adopter categories' shown in Fig. 8. It has been found that consumers who are among the first to adopt, especially the 'Early Adopters', have an influence on the later adopters, who seek information and guidance from friends and acquaintances who are already using the product (or service).

1. See answer to question 27 for full discussion of Product Life Cycle.

These Early Adopters act as 'opinion leaders' or 'influentials' in what is described as 'two-step flow of communications'. The two-step flow hypotheis is that communications do not flow straight from the mass media (including advertising) to all consumers, but that certain consumers (opinion leaders) absorb the information first and then transmit and interpret it to family, friends and social acquaintances. An example of this 'word-of-mouth' communication' would be an Early or Late Majority adopter who is considering the purchase of a quartz watch seeking the opinion of an Early Adopter who already has one.

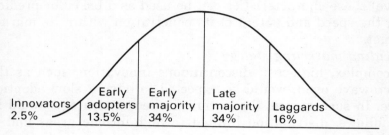

Fig. 8

3. Marketing and the Diffusion of Innovations

Diffusion theory appears useful to marketing managers in three ways:

(a) *Influencing opinion leaders*, and thus providing opportunities for increased sales.

(b) *Predicting adoption rates*, and thus assisting the sales forecast.

(c) *Deciding marketing strategy*.

Influencing opinion leaders

Unfortunately, opinion leaders are difficult to identify and contact. They are not the same people for all products, and their demographic and lifestyle characteristics are very similar to those of the later adopters who seek their advice. Further, some studies have concluded that their influence on purchase is limited, often merely confirming decisions that are on the point of being taken.

Nevertheless, practical attempts can be made to reach opinion leaders. One method is through media selection, for example advertising a new camera in the specialist photographic magazines likely to be read by opinion leaders. Alternatively, but more expensively, more general mass media such as television and national press can be used, with advertisements designed to attract and interest opinion leaders.

Predicting adoption

Successful and rapidly adopted innovations have certain characteristics. The most important of these are the innovation's advantages, relative to existing products, its conspicuousness in use, its simplicity and ease of understanding and cost. The extent to which the innovation has (or does not have) these characteristics can be used as a basis for predicting the speed and extent of its penetration within its market target.

Deciding marketing stategy

A complex, high-cost, discontinuous innovation, such as the microwave oven, would be expected to have a slow adoption rate. In such a case, the initial marketing strategy would be as follows: distribution limited to high-income areas and to outlets such as department stores that specialise in displaying and demonstrating expensive and modern domestic appliances; advertising placed in media that reaches young modern people, particularly women; price does not have to be low as those consumers wishing to buy a microwave oven at this stage of the diffusion process are able and willing to pay high prices.

In contrast, for a low-cost discontinuous innovation such as a soap powder, the expectation would be to obtain maximum trial and adoption as quickly as possible throughout the market. Therefore, distribution would be very extensive, with mass-media advertising and introductory low-price offers and promotions.

4. Conclusion

Consumers adopt new products at varying speeds. One of the factors determining this speed, especially of products that are indeed novel, is communication between consumers. While there is no doubt that such communication takes place, there is less certainty about the importance of this influence on purchasing and of how to reach the opinion-leading Early Adopters.

1. Definition of Market Segmentation

Market segmentation is the subdividing of a market into distinct subsets of customers, where any subset can be selected as a target market that can be reached by and will respond to a distinct Marketing Mix. Market segmentation derives from the concepts that:

(a) While all consumers are unique in their wants there is sufficient similarity between *some* to produce similarity in their wants; and

(b) a company is unlikely to be able to satisfy all customers in any one market.

Therefore, it is more profitable to concentrate on seeking large shares of fewer markets rather than to dissipate efforts by seeking small shares of all markets. By increasing understanding of the markets being served, market segmentation allows companies to 'tailor' their marketing activities more accurately and responsively to customer needs.

Segmenting consumer markets enables the company to improve the speed and accuracy with which it can:

(a) Uncover market opportunities by identifying gaps between consumer needs and the availability of suitable products or services.

(b) Adjust current Marketing Mixes to meet consumer requirements.

Obviously, there have to be limits to segmentation and, to be useful, market segments must first be *profitable*, by virtue of sales levels and margins available, and secondly *accessible*, through both advertising media and channels of distribution.

2. Bases for Segmenting Markets

Markets are segmented by classifying consumers in terms of a range of variables which indicate relative consumption preferences and patterns. The major variables are:

(a) *Market*: *Industrial* – those who purchase for resale or for use in the production of further goods and services; *Consumer* – those who purchase for direct consumption.

(b) *Demographic*: Physical and factual data on the consumer, principally age, sex, income, occupation, marital status, family size and cycle, Terminal Education Age (TEA), race and religion.

(c) *Psychographic*: Lifestyle, e.g. healthy, sporty, fashionable, traditional.

(d) *Geographic*: Urban, rural, inland, coastal, North, South.

(e) *Benefit sought*: e.g. convenience, economy, social prestige.

(f) *User status*: Heavy user, light, lapsed, occasional.

(g) *Marketing factor sensitivity*: Responsiveness to quality price, service, advertising.

(h) *'New' variables*: Being developed – SAGACITY, ACORN.[1]

3. Product Differentiation and Targeting

Market segmentation is often contrasted with product differentiation. Which is the introduction of differential features, quality, style or image with the objective that some consumers will perceive the product as superior and consequently prefer it when purchasing. In other words, this is the process of *branding*, examples of which can be seen in markets as diverse as groceries (Heinz baked beans) cigarettes, (Benson and Hedges) and cars (Range Rover).

As can be seen from these examples, product differentiation is the implementation of market segmentation, whereby products are developed to meet the needs of various types of consumer. This process is also referred to as 'target marketing' or 'targeting'. It must be noted that there is a fundamental distinction between market segmentation, which deals with the analysis of consumers and markets, and product differentiation/targeting, which are marketing strategies based on the analysis.

4. Segmentation of the Breakfast Cereal Market

This market can be usefully segmented by industrial/consumer demography, benefit sought, lifestyle and marketing factor sensitivity.

Industrial Market

Initially, the market should be segmented between *industrial* and *consumer* buyers. *Industrial* buyers such as hotels and hospitals require low price, reliable, fast delivery and good

1. For a full discussion of these variables, see answer to question 16.

dependable quality. Purchasing will be determined largely by this type of objective factor with little importance given to advertising and branding.

Demography

In *consumer markets*, *demographic* variables, especially family size and cycle will be important; large families containing young children will tend to be the heaviest purchasers with mothers requiring economy, convenience and nourishment, and the children preferring sweet taste and ease of eating. Socio-economic grade is unlikely to be an important segmentation variable – purchase of breakfast cereals is fairly evenly spread over all classes of large families.

Benefits sought

The various *benefits* sought are likely to be nourishment and economy, as mentioned above, and benefits based on lifestyles such as fitness, slimming and health.

Marketing factor sensitivity

The effect of this segmentation variable is indicated by the differing reactions of buyers to heavily advertised products, lower-priced own-brands, and promotions.

5. Segmentation of the Diesel Engine Market

This is essentially, if not exclusively, an industrial market which can be segmented in terms of geography, end-use markets, customer size, Decision Making Unit and criteria used in purchasing.

Geography

Geographical segmentation can be useful for organisational reasons, but is also likely to reflect differing requirements in terms of climate, performance, price and possibly conformity to environmental standards.

End-use market

Given that diesel engines will be installed by purchasers into their own products, the end-use markets into which these finished products go are likely to influence requirements. Therefore, it would be useful to segment according to road haulage (trucks) personal transport (cars), passenger transport (buses), agricultural equipment, boats, and so on.

Customer size

This will affect usage rate and importance to the supplier and will require (and justify) different levels of delivery and service.

Decision Making Unit

The Decision Making Units involved in purchasing in organisations vary in composition and authority. For example, in some cases the Chief Engineer might be of particular importance whereas in others this role might be taken by the Accountant or Managing Director, or authority might be evenly shared. This type of segmentation will assist the engine manufacturer to design the sales and marketing strategies most likely to be successful.

Benefits sought

Rather like consumers, industrial buyers differ in their *buying objectives* (or *benefits sought*) and diesel engine buyers could be segmented according to the relative importance they ascribe to factors such as price, delivery, reliability, quality and so on.

6. Conclusion

Market segmentation is a consumer-oriented process. It is applicable to almost any type of market and provides a basis on which the company can develop appropriate products and strategies for selling and promotion.

Answer 15   **Socio-economic Grade**   Question page 3

1. Definition

Market segmentation is the subdividing of a market into distinct subsets of customers, where any subset may be selected as a target market which can be reached by, and will respond to, a distinct marketing mix. The concept of segmentation derives from the fact that while all consumers are unique in their wants there is sufficient similarity between *some* to produce similarity in their wants.

Market segmentation is used to discriminate between consumers to indicate relative purchasing power and consumption patterns.

The major criteria used for this discrimination in consumer markets[1] are:

(a) *Demographic*: Physical and factual data on the consumer, notably age, sex, income, occupation, marital status, family size and cycle, Terminal Education Age (TEA), race and religion.

(b) *Psychographic*: Lifestyle, e.g,. 'jet set' vs. 'stay-at-home'.

(c) *Benefit sought*: e.g. convenience, economy.

(d) *User status*: Heavy, light, lapsed.

(e) *Geographic*: Urban, rural, inland, coastal, North, South, neighbourhood type.

(f) *'New' variables*: Recently developed in UK: SAGACITY, based on an amalgam of life cycle and socio-economic grade; and ACORN, based on type of house whether owned or rented, and neighbourhood type

2. Applications of Socio-economic Grade to Market Segmentation

Of the segmentation variables, those under the demographic heading are the most used in marketing. And of the demographic variables, the most used are economic level and occupation, combined in the UK National Readership Survey into *Social Class* or *Socio-economic-grade* with the following categories.

(a) *Class A: The Upper-Middle Class* – successful business or professionals or with considerable private means, e.g. established solicitor, doctor, director-level executive or head of large school or college.

(b) *Class B: The Middle Class* – quite senior people, but below those in Class A, e.g. professionally qualified managers, accountants, surveyors, newly-qualified doctors and solicitors.

(c) *Class C$_1$: The Lower-Middle Class* – small tradespeople, 'white-collar workers', e.g. junior managerial, clerical workers, managers of small shops.

(d) *Class C$_2$: Skilled Workers* – e.g. bricklayers, carpenters, bus drivers, bakers.

(e) *Class D: Semi-skilled and Unskilled Workers* – labourers, postmen, milkmen.

(f) *Class E: Lowest Subsistence* – casual labourers and those

---

1. For a full discussion of these variables, see answer to question 14

dependent on state pensions, unemployment and supplementary benefits.

Such classification is used not only to differentiate the readership of newspapers, but also the purchase of a wide range of products and services, and reflects the commonly used and rather simplistic phrases 'up-market' (primarily ABC_1) and 'down-market' (C_2DE).

In 1983 the National Readership Survey estimated that the population of the United Kingdom was divided into socio-economic grades in the following proportions: AB 17%; C_1 22%; C_2 31%; D 18%; E 12%.

3. Segmentation by Socio-economic Grade

Inevitably, a classification system of this simplicity has limitations. First, take for example a 'C_2': this can be a man or a woman of any age and any interests and a purchaser of practically any product. For example, 16% of Times readers are C_2. Therefore, in order to discriminate between consumers in terms that reflect different purchasing patterns, it is necessary to use additional variables. Thus, it is possible to describe heavy users of lager as 'those C_2s who are also male and aged 18–34'. Similarly, the heavy users of whisky are 'those ABC_1s who are male and aged over 35'.

However, in some cases, socio-economic grade has no relation to purchasing. For example, purchasing of baked beans is distributed fairly equally over *all* socio-economic grades, and the factor that discriminates the heavy user is the presence of young children; provided that the household contains children aged under 15, it is highly probable that the housewife will be a major buyer of baked beans, regardless of socio-economic grade. Again, buyers in the same socio-economic grade (and in the same demographic profile in general) often differ widely in their purchasing. For example, socio-economic grade does not discriminate between buyers of branded and private-label baked beans, or between AB males of 35 plus who are heavy drinkers of whisky and those who are light or non-drinkers. In these and many other cases, it is necessary to undertake further segmentation by lifestyle.

A second criticism of socio-economic grade is that it fails to distinguish the levels of disposable income available to households of the same grade. Compare, for example, a bus driver with no children whose wife works, with another who is married with three school-aged children.

A third criticism is that socio-economic grade is determined by the occupation of the head of the household, usually the husband. However, working housewives might have C_1 office jobs, but be married to a C_2 manual worker. Although this is unlikely to cause confusion to the household, it does present a problem to the market-research executive deciding on classification.

A fourth problem arises from misuse of the concept. Whereas socio-economic grade is based on occupation, it is usually interpreted in terms of a hierarchy of income. However, this becomes inaccurate in cases such as C_2 lorry drivers having a greater income than C_1 teachers.

Fifth, there is a research methodology problem. Socio-economic classification is based on the occupation of the head of the household, but frequently the data are collected not from that person but from another member of the family who might be unable or unwilling to give an accurate answer. The existence and extent of this problem is demonstrated by the variations in the proportions of the economic grades found by the different surveys, JICNARS and TGI[2]

4. Conclusion
Despite the many criticisms, socio-economic grade remains a highly used segmentation variable. Provided that it is not used in markets where it is inappropriate and is augmented by other relevant segmentation criteria, it is very useful in analysing markets and designing marketing campaigns.

Answer 16   ACORN and SAGACITY   Question page 4

---

1. Market Segmentation
Market segmentation is the subdividing of a market into distinct subsets of customers, where any subset may be selected as a target market which can be reached by, and will respond to, a distinct marketing mix. The concept of segmentation de-

---

2 Respectively, Joint Industry Committee for National Readership Surveys, and Target Group Index.

rives from the fact that while all consumers are unique in their wants there is sufficient similarity between *some* to produce similarity in their wants. Market segmentation is used to discriminate between consumers to indicate differences in purchasing power and consumption patterns.

The traditional segmentation variables of demographics, psychographics, geography and benefits sought have been criticised in their descriptive powers of many markets. ACORN and SAGACITY are two variables, based on demography, that have been developed by market researchers in the United Kingdom to overcome these shortcomings.

2. ACORN
ACORN has been developed by the research company CACI and is an acronym for 'A Classification Of Residential Neighbourhoods'. Its central idea is that a set of areas shown by the Census of the Registrar-General to have similar demographic and social characteristics will, as a result, share common lifestyle features and thus present similar potential for the sales of any product. The purpose of ACORN is to define these different sets of areas and to show where, within Great Britain, they can be found.

This is done by classifying the 125,000 'enumeration districts' (the smallest voting ward) of the census into thirty-six 'neighbourhood types', such as 'Mixed housing, young families' (ACORN Code 2), 'Modern private housing, high income' (Code 30), 'Recent council housing' (Code 3) and 'Areas of elderly people, flats and homes' (Code 36). For many purposes it has been found that thirty-six neighbourhood types provide an unnecessarily fine level of detail, the types are reduced to the alternative form of eleven groups, such as 'Modern family housing for manual workers' (Group A), 'Urban local authority housing' (Group F) and 'Traditional high-status suburbia', (Group J).

The ACORN types and groups are created from 40 variables, mostly traditionally demographic, but supplemented with others such as the proportion of married females working, owner-occupier, number of rooms per person and frequency of moving house. Thus, ACORN discriminates in much more detail than do demographic variables when used alone. For example, it has shown that whilst Esher and Hampstead are similar in terms of socio-economic grade, purchasing patterns differ considerably. Similar differences between districts of equivalent socio-economic grade have been found, not only within the UK, e.g. Basildon and Bethnal Green, but also within other countries where ACORN has been applied. When used in conjunction with other market research information from Target Group Index, the National Readership Survey or AGB panels, ACORN can indicate major differences between areas in terms of readership, purchasing and saving. ACORN can assist in decisions such as:

(a) the location of new retail outlets
(b) which products to stock in which areas
(c) addresses for mail-outs
(d) the selection of samples.

ACORN is particularly applicable in the targeting of products that are related specifically to the house or home, e.g. gardening equipment and supplies, home improvements such as double glazing and do-it-yourself products.

3. SAGACITY

The term 'SAGACITY' is taken presumably to indicate that its creators Research Services Limited consider it 'mentally penetrating, gifted with discernment'. Using the JICNARS National Readership Survey, SAGACITY is an attempt to refine the standard socio-economic classifications by further demographic subdivision according to life cycle and disposable income. This gives twelve groupings, as shown in Fig. 9.

The terms used in the chart have the following meanings.

Dependent: Informants still living in their parents' household.

Pre-family: Adults under 35, established in their own household but with no children.

Family: Housewives and heads of households under 65 with one or more children aged under 21 in the household.

Late: All other adults over 35 and childless or whose children have left home.

Better/worse off: Are descriptions of income level of *both head of household and spouse*.

White/Blue: ABC_1 and $C_2 DE$ respectively.

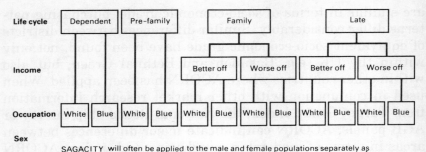

Life cycle	Dependent		Pre-family		Family				Late			
Income					Better off		Worse off		Better off		Worse off	
Occupation	White	Blue	White	Blue	White	Blue	White	Blue	White	Blue	White	Blue
Sex												

SAGACITY will often be applied to the male and female populations separately as in the published tables.

Source: *Sagacity: A special analysis of JICNARS NRS data*, undertaken by Research Services Limited

Fig. 9

Because of its multivariable base, SAGACITY provides a more accurate description than traditional segmentation variables over a wide range of markets. By including a number of variables, SAGACITY permits researchers to examine fairly small differences in usership (and non-usership) of a product and also to relate these categories of consumers to the National Readership Survey.

For example, SAGACITY shows that a Pre-family, White (collar) consumer takes nearly twice as many overseas package holidays as a Pre-family Blue (collar) consumer. Similar analyses are possible for the purchase of consumer durables, bank account holding, readership and other products.

4. Conclusion

Both ACORN and SAGACITY are fairly new approaches to segmentation, and both have been developed by research companies, whereas the sources of previous variables were generally non-commercial. For many markets, they do appear to offer promising bases as a result of their multivariate nature and relationship to the problems and requirements of marketing.

Answer 17   Market Research Design   Question page 4

1. Definition and Scope of Market Research
Market research is the collection, analysis and interpretation

of information about consumers, products, competitors and other environmental factors, with the purpose of providing guidance and risk reduction in the taking of marketing decisions.

Market research provides information on market size and potential; the market share and strengths and weaknesses (especially as perceived by consumers) of brands; consumers' buying habits, requirements and usage; the nature and effect of advertising strategy, price levels and distribution; and the activities of competitors. Market research can produce both qualitative data, which explores and diagnoses the nature and elements of market, and *quantitative* data, which informs about the size, shape, proportions and incidence of the characteristics of markets. Market research can be both *continuous* and *ad hoc*, and covers marketing topics such as market size and share, price setting; packaging, distribution and the development and assessment of products and advertising. In all market-research exercises there are certain stages to the market-research process.

(a) *Problem definition*: A statement of the topic to be researched.
(b) *Research design*: A specification of the data to be collected, the methods to be used for its collection, and, where appropriate, a sampling plan.
(c) *Data collection*: The process of contacting and questioning respondents and the examination of other sources of information to be used.
(d) *Data analysis*: The organisation of the data collected into information that is meaningful and relevant to the problem.
(e) *Report presentation and recommendations*: the account of the research – objectives, methodology, findings and suggestions for action.

2. Market Research for Proposed Range of Infant Foods

Decisions such as entry to new markets and the manufacture of new products require extensive and thorough research because of their complexity and the risk involved, and it is certain that a major research agency would be employed.

However, the stages of the research should be as described above and applied in the following manner.

Problem definition

The problem is to investigate the feasibility of the company's entry to the infant-food market. This requires an estimate of market size and potential and an analysis of any gap that would offer the company substantial sales. It is necessary to assess the market needs in terms of the company's resources and strengths, i.e. its capacity to make and market the products and to meet distribution and promotion requirements.

Research design

As this is a major research project, covering all aspects of marketing and the market, a wide range of data and research techniques is necessary. Information on present and past market size and shares, penetration and advertising levels is likely to be available from *secondary sources* – data already existing, such as AGB, Nielsen and MEAL. However, to analyse consumers in terms of demographic profile, the influences on their purchasing, e.g. advertising, hospital, health visitor, mother, their usage of and attitudes towards infant food requires a User and Attitude study – a form of *primary research*, i.e. the collection of data not presently available.

The Usage and Attitude study involves the selection of samples of the target market, probably by a quota sample. The first stage is *qualitative research* of a fairly small sample – say 60–80 by group discussions and/or individually by depth interviews (or use of Kelly grids) to elicit 'consumer language',[1] salient attitudes and influences on purchase. As the infant food market is still developing and because the product is emotive, it might be decided to undertake an observational study in a sample of shops to examine how mothers actually buy the product. Having discovered from qualitative research how consumers behave in the market and the attitudes they hold, *quantitative* research is then used to ascribe numerical importance to these findings. For example, the number of con-

1. 'Consumer language' consists of the terms used by consumers rather than those used by manufacturers and the trade. For example, it is highly likely that young mothers use the term 'baby food' rather than the more technical 'infant food'.

sumers who prefer say glass containers to tins, the levels of sweetness preferred, the number of consumers to whom convenience is important, the number who were influenced in their purchase by health visitors.

For the quantitative research, a much larger sample is used – 300–1,000 – depending on the range and complexity of the data collected at the qualitative stage, and the action standards imposed. Once again, the sample should be selected to be representative of the target group. The quantitative information is collected by questionnaire, administered by an interviewer. As this questionnaire is likely to be fairly long, and might well include some element of product testing, street interviewing is not practical. In addition, as the respondents are mothers of very young children, a central location for the interviews is also inappropriate.

Therefore, the cost of home-administered questionnaires is justified. As the completed questionnaires will require statistical analysis, it is essential that the design includes the required precoding.

Data analysis

As indicated above, the qualitative data is analysed prior to, and as a basis for, the quantitative research. The quantitative data for such a large study requires the use of computer-based statistical techniques.

Report and recommendations

A familiar type of comment about market research is that in the dark it does not show which way to go, but it can provide very good lighting. It is essential that the Research Report shows the scope and methodology of the study undertaken, as these determine the quality and usefulness of the conclusions and recommendations.

Conclusions should specify the opportunities and requirements of the market and the recommendations should suggest action, such as 'Market entry with a described product range, with specified prices, promotion and distribution'.

However, before the launch of any products, the company needs to undertake further research on the development of products, packaging and advertising strategies, as well as a Test Market.

1. Sampling in Market Research

Samples are representative selections of larger aggregations or populations and are used in all types of market research from *ad hoc* product tests to continuous surveys such as the measurement of television audiences. Sampling is an essential ingredient of market research, as it is almost always impractical to investigate the attitudes and behaviour of every consumer in a market. Apart from the cost, the data would almost certainly be out of date by the time they were collected and analysed. (The possible exceptions are to be found in very specialised industrial markets, such as heavy aircraft, where there are few customers all spending large amounts of money.)

Therefore, by sampling a relatively small number of people, it is possible to concentrate efforts towards ensuring that the data collected are accurate. Properly conducted, sampling produces results that are just as good as those from a (very fast) census.

2. Standard Error

The accuracy of sample results (as estimates of a population's characteristics) depend on the representativeness of the sample. This is determined by the size of the sample and the variability of the population. Good results are not dependent on taking a large sample, and if a population were completely homogeneous, regardless of its size, a sample of one would provide a perfectly accurate representation. However, in market research, populations are not homogeneous. For example, annual household expenditure on overseas holidays might range from zero to £10,000; and weekly individual television viewing from zero to 56 hours. When sampling to ascertain *average* annual household expenditure on overseas holidays, or *average* annual TV viewing, it is impossible to know whether respondents are concentrated near one extreme rather than evenly distributed over the entire range.

The extent to which the sample average or mean can be relied on as a guide to the population mean can be measured by the *standard error*, calculated with the following equation:

$$\frac{S}{\sqrt{n}}$$

where: S = standard deviation of the sample mean (i.e. an indication of the population's variability).

and: n = sample size.

Thus, for the overseas holiday example, the sample data might give a mean of £1,100 with a standard deviation of £400 from a sample of 625.

Therefore,

$$\text{standard error} = \frac{£400}{\sqrt{625}}$$
$$= £16$$

From this it can be stated that there is a 68% probability that the population mean is within the band £1,084 and £1,116, i.e. one standard error. If a 95% probability (the level most used in market research) is required, it is necessary to allow two standard errors. Thus, there is a 95% probability that the average annual household expenditure on overseas holidays is between £1,068 and £1,132.

The range of error can be reduced by increasing the sample size, but in order to *halve* the error it is necessary to *quadruple* the size of the sample:

$$\frac{£400}{\sqrt{2,500}} = £8$$

Standard error can be used in relation to sample estimates expressed in percentages, using the formula:

$$\sqrt{\frac{p(100-p)}{n}}$$

where: p = % found

For example, if, with a sample of 625 it is found that 10% of the population surveyed take an annual overseas holiday, the standard error of this estimate is:

$$\sqrt{\frac{10 \times 90}{625}} \simeq 1.2\%$$

Thus, there is a 95% probability that between 7.6% and 12.4% of the population surveyed take an annual overseas holiday. In these examples a sample of 625 gives a range for average expenditure that is much more likely to be acceptable than the range for the percentage and in this latter case it is probable that a larger sample would be taken.

Provided that in advance some reasonable estimate can be made of the standard deviation of the population to be surveyed, it is possible to decide the size of the sample required to achieve given levels of accuracy.

3. Non-random Sampling

While random sampling fulfils the statistical criteria for representing the population accurately, it is rarely used in market research because of its cost and impracticality, as it requires that each and every member of the drawn sample is interviewed. Therefore, when using non-random sampling it is invalid, in the strictest statistical terms, to use the standard error techniques to measure the accuracy of sample estimates. In practice, however, the standard error techniques can be used with carefully selected non-random samples to produce helpful indications of the accuracy of the sample estimate.

4. Bias

Bias in the selection of the sample can occur with any sampling method. One source is the sampling frame (the list from which the sample is selected). Typically used sampling frames are electoral lists and companies' mailing or customer lists. If the list used is incomplete or inaccurate in some other way, the result is that not all members of the population have an equal chance of selection. Clearly, it is essential to take all steps to ensure that lists used are up to date and accurate.

A second source of bias is non-response. Some members of a random sample are certain to be unobtainable, and for both random and non-random samples it is equally certain that there will be refusals. Moreover, the reasons for this non-response might be very relevant to the objectives of the survey. There is the anecdote about the poor response to a postal questionnaire to dog-owners because the dogs had destroyed the questionnaires on arrival. There are more frequent problems, such as locating respondents who spend very long periods at work, and in obtaining co-operation from respondents like young mothers who are busy, or old people who might be nervous. In all cases, the very causes of response and non-response might bias the results. For example, it is often said that the sort of people who are prepared to attend hall-tests have different lifestyle characteristics to refusers. Non-response can be minimised by the use of well-trained and supervised interviewers.

A third form of bias is that caused by interviewers – 'interviewer bias'. On quota samples this can arise from the selection of respondents, as interviewers tend to prefer those who are easier to contact and whose manner and appearance they find attractive. While this can never be eliminated, it can be reduced by interviewer training and the use of controls, such as placing limits on the number of the more accessible respondents to be interviewed.

5. Conclusion
Sampling involves decisions and compromises between practical and academic objectives. By the use of care and controls it is possible to obtain the advantages of sampling without unacceptable loss of accuracy.

Answer 19   **Sampling Methods**   Question page 4

(a) Probability Sampling
A probability sample, or random sample, is one in which every member of the population being sampled has a known and equal chance of being selected. This selection can be done by ascribing a number to each member of the population and drawing from these numbers at random (for example, by using a table of random numbers) until the sample has been filled. Alternatively, the sample can be filled *systematically* by drawing the first member at random from a numbered list, and then drawing the remainder of the sample at the appropriate numbered interval. Thus, for a sample of 10 from a population of 1000, if the first number chosen is 721, the other sample members will be numbers 821, 921, 21 and so on.

A *stratified random sample* is one where a population that is heterogeneous is divided into categories or strata whose relative size are known, for example socio-economic grade. Within each stratum a sample, proportionate to the stratum's relative size, is randomly selected.

While probability sampling fulfils the statistical criteria for representing the population accurately, it is expensive and often impractical, as it necessitates interviewing each and every member of the drawn sample. Even if there are sufficient funds and time to locate every member of the sample, there can never be any guarantee that everyone will agree to co-operate.

Because of these problems random sampling is not frequently used in market research projects. The main exception is the National Readership Survey, which uses an annual random sample of 30,000 individuals aged 15 or over.

(b) Cluster Sampling

Cluster sampling is one of the major modifications of the simple random sample. It is the process whereby interviews are not spread throughout the population but are concentrated within geographical areas, for example a restricted number of constituencies or administrative districts. It is used for practicality, because of the considerable savings it offers, in comparison with sampling completely at random, due to the reduction in interviewers' travelling. The extent to which clustering reduces the accuracy of the sample estimates depends on the number and size of the clusters used and their homogeneity.

(c) Quota Sampling

This is the most commonly used type of non-random sampling in market research, with the selection of respondents made by the interviewer within guidelines. The client company or the research agency usually knows the profile of the population that uses the product being researched and matches the sample accordingly. For example, if 50% of lager drinkers are male C_2, 30% are male DE and 20% are male ABC_1, then on a sample of 100 the interviewer is instructed to interview 50 C_2 males, 30 DE males and 20 ABC_1 males. In practice, of course, the segmentation represented by the quota is far more complex than in this example. Quota sampling offers great savings compared to random sampling in terms of cost and speed. At the planning stage there is no need to select names and addresses and at the fieldwork stage anyone within the quota description is eligible for interview, so it is not necessary to track down specific individuals.

However, the quota method has the major disadvantage that the choice of respondents can be biased according to their availability, willingness to co-operate and the tendency of interviewers to prefer to speak to people whose appearance they find attractive. While this can never be eliminated, it can be reduced by interviewer training and the use of controls, such as placing limits on the number of the more accessible respondents, e.g. married non-working women, or white-collar workers. A further disadvantage arising from this non-random sampling is that, strictly, it is invalid to use statistical techniques to measure sampling errors. In practice however, the techniques are used, as it is essential to have some measurement of the accuracy of sample estimates.

(d) Multiphase Sampling
A survey often measures more than one factor; for example purchasing behaviour *and* attitudes in respect of a market or product group. Because of the data or accuracy required, or because of the characteristics of the population, it might be that 1,000 interviews are necessary to obtain the necessary product data, whreas only 500 are sufficient to meet the requirements of the attitude data. Therefore, to economise in both the fieldwork and the data processing, the purchasing part of the questionnaire can be put to all 1,000 respondents, and the attitude part to alternate respondents only.

(e) Disproportionate Sampling
Frequently, researchers are particularly interested in the attitudes or behaviour of certain sub-sections of the population sampled. If these constitute small proportions of the population, it is necessary to take a very big sample in order to obtain sufficient questionnaires for useful analysis. This can be avoided by biasing the sample disproportionately towards the sub-section required. For example, a study of smokers' toothpaste (a product with very low market penetration) might require users and non-users, and select respondents so that the two groups are equally represented. It is essential that at the analysis stage the proportions as represented in the population are restored.

1. Sources of Inaccuracy

Questionnaires are a major element in the collection of market research data on the behaviour and attitudes of consumers. The objective of using a questionnaire is to obtain the information sought with the maximum accuracy and the minimum cost. There are numerous potential causes of inaccuracy, not least that the wrong people might be questioned – for example, the wrong age group, or beer-only drinkers when wine drinkers are required. Further, the respondents who agree to answer might be unrepresentative of the population being researched. Even with the right respondents, inaccuracies can occur.

(a) The respondent might misunderstand the questions, because of ambiguity or the use of words or terms with which he is not familiar.

(b) The respondent might know the answer, but be unable to verbalise it, especially if it relates to attitudes or if the respondent is inarticulate.

(c) The respondent might have known the answer once, but has since forgotten, for example the date when a product was last purchased.

(d) The respondent might give an unconsidered answer, due to tiredness or boredom.

(e) The respondent might know the answer, but be unwilling to reveal it, as he or she feels that it is embarassing, self-critical or impolite. Typical examples are questions on age, income and personal habits.

(f) The respondent's answer might be subject to 'interviewer bias' – the interviewer overtly leading the respondent towards a certain answer, or the respondent giving answers which he feels will please or impress the interviewer.

2. General Functions of Questionnaires

While each questionnaire must be designed for the particular research study, it must also fulfil six general functions in order to be effective:

(a) *Maintain the respondent's co-operation and involvement*: It must not be boring or exhausting. This can be achieved by restricting the length and by sequencing so that questions that are mundane or require 'thought' are spaced between others that are more interesting.

(b) *Communicate with the correspondent*: Avoid ambiguity, unnecessary complexity and abstract and vague concepts.

(c) *Help the respondent to work out his answers*: Allow some generalising, avoid the need for prodigious feats of memory, for example by use of prompt cards and multiple-choice answers.

(d) *Avoid bias*: Ensure that questions do not lead to particular answers, for example, do not word a question as follows: 'We have found that most people brush their teeth three times a day. How often do you brush yours?' Also the questionnaire should not encourage personalisation by the interviewer.

(e) *Make the interviewer's task as easy as possible*: Use clear layout, large, legible type and as simple a structure as possible.

(f) *Provide an efficient basis for data processing*: Use a layout that allows data to be transferred direct to the computer for analysis. As many questions as possible should be 'closed', i.e. respondent given a choice of predetermined coded answers.

Points (a)–(e) are concerned mainly with the accuracy of the information collected and point (f) with minimising cost and time.

3. Sequencing and Presentation of Questions

A major influence on the accuracy of data collected is the sequence of questions. Easily-answered, non-controversial questions, such as 'Do you have a cat?' or 'Do you ever do any decorating at home?' should be placed first. Such questions relax the respondent and can also screen out those who are not in the target group. More personal and potentially embarassing questions, such as those on age or income, can be more easily answered later in the questionnaire when some confidence and rapport has been established.

Answers to some personal questions can be encouraged also by asking respondents to indicate ranges or tick boxes, rather than give the information specifically and verbally. For

example, for age a card can be shown on which there are intervals 16–24, 25–34, 35–44 and so on.

4. Behavioural Information

Many surveys require information on the type of consumer
who buys a product, when and where they buy it and how it
is used. Respondents often have trouble in remembering these
details accurately, and they can be assisted by specifying the
product accurately, e.g. 'wholemeal' rather than 'brown' bread
or, in the consumers' language, 'Martini-type drink' rather
than 'vermouth'. Further, they can be asked to think carefully
and for some time before replying to questions such as 'how
many loaves of wholemeal bread do you buy in a normal
week?'

More accurate answers will be obtained if questions are
broken down into constituent parts. For example, instead of
asking 'On what occasions do you drink Martini?' ask:

Do you drink Martini at any of the following times?:
Midday . . . . .
Evening . . . . .
At home . . . . .
In pubs . . . . .
At parties . .
With meals . .
Other occasions

5. Attitudinal Information

Attitudes, or what people *feel* about objects, are difficult to
measure for several reasons. First, it is necessary to measure
not only the existence of the attitude, but also its *strength*; for
example, 'How fashionable are X brand of jeans?' or 'How
hard-wearing are Y brand of shoes?' Second, it is necessary to
measure the *importance* of the attitude to the consumer when
purchasing. For example, a car buyer might well have attitudes on a car's economy and its easily adjusted door-mirror.
However it is very likely that the former has a much greater
influence when deciding to buy. Third, it is difficult to measure attitudes, especially their relative importance, without
leading the respondent.

There are various ways that questionnaire design can reduce such problems. Opened-ended questions, such as 'What

are the best things about drinking Martini?' can indicate which attitudes are important. Indirect questions, using scales, give information that is easy to measure and process. For example,

Martini is drunk mainly by:
Younger people   Older people

Simpler attitudes can be measured by *numerical* scales, for example strength of an alcoholic drink on a scale of 1 to 10; or by semantic differential scales, for example,

Strong   Weak

6. Piloting

Regardless of the experience of the researcher, the care with which the principles of questionnaire design are applied and the time constraints, it is essential that the questionnaire is piloted, i.e. that the proposed format is tried out on a small sample, to assess that its objectives are being achieved. It is at this stage that unexpected problems of ambiguity, incomprehen sion and excessive length can be identified and rectified at much less cost than if undetected until completion of the survey.

Answer 21   **Retail Audits and Consumer Panels**   Question page 5

---

1. Introduction

Retail audits and consumer panels are methods for the continuous research of sales and purchasing, using samples of retail outlets and consumers respectively.

2. Retail Audits

The name that is often synonymous with retail auditing is A. C. Nielsen Co. Ltd, whose 'Food Index', 'Drug Index', 'Confectionery Index' and Liquor Index' and, more recently, 'DIY Index', provide information that is essential to the planning of many companies. However, in the UK a number of other companies also operate retail audits in specialist food and non-food markets, for example Retail Audits Limited.

The retail audit is based on samples of retail outlets through which the products being monitored are sold. Thus, the principal forms of retail outlet covered are grocers, chemists and CTNs (Confectionery, Tobacco and Newsagent Shops)

Sales of each outlet are measured by comparing deliveries in the period with opening and closing stock levels. The 'audit cycle' or frequency of measurement varies from weekly for the RAL cigarette audit to bi-monthly for the Nielsen audits, except for DIY which is quarterly. Sales totals by volume and sterling value are provided for each product group covered and also broken down to show branch shares and sales by type of outlet and TV area. There is further information on retailer stock levels, retail selling prices, distribution levels, out-of-stock, promotions and display. Manufacturers buy data as they require, usually referring to the product areas in which they are operating.

Retail audit data, particularly the Drug Index, is valuable to a toiletries company in a number of ways. In the short term, knowledge of brand shares helps in the assessment of the effect on sales of its advertising and promotional campaigns and those of its competitors. Information on sales through various types of outlet and the display and prices of its products in all outlets can indicate where and what action is needed over distribution.

In the longer term, retail audit data show the trends in market sizes and brand shares within markets and thus assist in decision-making on product mix and development, pricing and advertising. For example, developments in markets such as health foods would be shown by the retail audit and cause the company to consider diversification.

Inevitably there are criticisms of the retail audit system, the most significant of which is that the samples used cannot be representative, because it has been impossible for any audit company to obtain the co-operation of all large multiple grocers or of Marks and Spencer and Boots. Obviously this could be of major importance to a toiletries company, and allowances would be necessary when interpreting data. Also the number of retail outlets is constantly changing, yet retail audit companies up-date their sample only every two or three years, with consequential interruptions to trend data.

A further criticism arises from the bi-monthly cycle of most retail audits, which is satisfactory to represent trend data, but might be too infrequent for a seasonal product. This could affect toiletry products such as those related to suntanning, Christmas presents and cough and cold treatments.

Retail audits are costly, because of the fieldwork involved in covering a very wide range of outlets and products. The final report is made several weeks after fieldwork is finished, in which time the market can have changed.

The development of EPOS (electronic point-of-sale) equipment should lead to a substantial improvement. Computerised stock control and electronic tills linked to computers will provide sales data on a daily, even hourly basis, without the need for expensive fieldwork.

3. Consumer Panels

Consumer panels are based on a representative sample of individuals or households drawn from the population being studied. They measure aspects of behaviour, ranging from purchasing to television viewing. The measurement is continuous over the full period of the study. Some panels, such as that for television audience measurement, are permanent with a phased change of membership, while others are short-term, for example to test a new product.

In the UK, the purchase of household consumer goods is measured by the Attwood Consumer Panel and the Home Audit and TCA (Television Consumer Audit) of AGB; television viewing, of both ITV and BBC, is measured by the BARB (Broadcasters' Audience Research Board) operated by AGB. There are also panels for motoring purchases (petrol, oil and accessories) and for agricultural purchases. However, the three panels of particular interest to a toiletries company are AGB's TCPI (Toiletries, Cosmetics Personal Index) RSGB's Baby Panel and Attwoods AMSAC panel.

The methods of data collection used by these panels vary between *postal diaries* (Attwood, TCPI and Motorists'); *homes audits*, by fieldworkers of purchases and used packs (TCA) and interviewers plus diary (Baby Panel). The postal diary is obviously relatively inexpensive and, in addition, the diary can collect data on unbranded products and foodstuffs bought loose that are more likely to be missed by the home audit.

Consumer panels give information on the consumer structure of a market. They show the level of market penetration (the proportion of consumers buying the product) the amounts they buy and at what intervals, degrees of brand loyalty, direction of brand switching, consumers' perceptions of what contitute substitutes; and the type of buyer, segmented by demographics.

Thus the panel would tell the company whether a 10% market share for one of its brands (as reported by Nielsen) means that 10% of consumers in the market are regular buyers or whether a smaller proportion of buyers are heavy users.

Such information can be used as a basis for marketing activity. For example, sales concentrated among a small number of consumers (i.e. low penetration) might indicate the need for a promotional campaign to increase awareness among non-users. Alternatively, a high level of penetration but with extensive brand switching, might lead to a campaign to increase brand loyalty.

The toiletries manufacturer or its advertising agency would, like all TV advertisers, make use of the viewing data produced from the BARB panel. In addition, it might well use short-term panels set up specifically for its own exclusive use to measure the effect of test marketing activity or to collect other information that is too specialised or complex for the syndicated panels.

4. TGI
A further syndicated survey on consumer usage of a wide range of products, that the toiletries company would undoubtedly use, is TGI (Target Group Index) operated by BMRB (British Market Research Bureau Ltd). TGI also includes information on media usage. However, as it is not panel based, it is only mentioned here.

5. Need for Both Types of Panel
It is clear that both retail audits and consumer panels are necessary to the toiletries manufacturer because each provides different sorts of data. Retail audits show *where* the product is being bought, its market share and those of its competitors,

the display it and its competitors are getting, and the promotional activity in the market.

Consumer panels show *who* is buying the product and the pattern of this purchasing.

---

1. The Scope of Qualitative and Quantitative Research

The function of consumer research is to obtain and process information about consumers that can assist in development and decision-making in the marketing and advertising of goods and services.

This description applies equally to quantitative and qualitative research, and the important difference between them lies in the type of information each provides and the methods by which this information is obtained.

In practice, qualitative research adds to the understanding of the nature and elements of consumers and markets; its information comes from asking What? How? and Why? Quantitative research informs about the size, shape and proportion of consumers and market characteristics, and comes from asking Who? Which? How many? and How important?

Quantitative research is usually based on large, carefully drawn samples; the data obtained are quantified and ascribed a degree of statistical significance. Conclusions are generalised to the population represented by the sample.

2. The Nature of Qualitative Research

Some research problems require a more flexible approach than can be provided by the standardised interviewing techniques, and often quantitative research cannot provide sufficient depth because its methods are of necessity structured. In these circumstances, qualitative research is employed to provide the necessary depth, subtlety and variety of information.

Qualitative research is usually exploratory or diagnostic. It involves small numbers of people who are not sampled on a probabilistic basis, although they may be selected to represent different categories of people from a given target market or community. No attempt is made to draw hard-and-fast conclusions and the results are impressionistic rather than definitive.

Qualitative research can obtain information in the following areas.

(a) Background information where absolutely nothing is known, for example, a completely new market.

(b) General problem definition and formulation of hypotheses for further investigation and quantification.

(c) Identification of relevant or salient behaviour patterns, beliefs, opinions, attitudes and motivations.

(d) Everyday consumer language used in relation to products, services and brands.

(e) Identification and exploration of new concepts for products or advertising themes.

3. Methods of Obtaining Qualitative Information

In qualitative research, respondents are interviewed, either individually or in small groups. The main types of interview are as follows.

Group discussion

The 'group' for a group discussion is a number of respondents brought together under the direction of a researcher acting as group leader. Usually, the number of respondents varies between five and eight but occasionally can be as many as twelve, depending on the amount of talking that is anticipated. ('Professional' people tend to talk a great deal; elderly people a lot less.)

The purpose is to cover a number of broad areas related to the problem being investigated, by having participants talk freely about their experiences, views, feelings and behaviour. For example, a group of housewives might be required to discuss problems of cleaning hard surfaces in the home, and the attributes of various products and brands available for this task.

Group discussions have the advantage of being a low-cost (compared to individual interviews) method of obtaining and comparing information on a wide range of consumer attitudes and behaviour. Further, as respondents heavily outnumber the researcher, the possibility of interviewer bias is minimised and respondents are more likely to speak and act naturally. Lastly, verbal interactions between respondents sharpen distinctions in attitudes and behaviour and demonstrate every-day consumer language.

However, the researcher's skill is necessary to avoid the dangers that a dominant personality might lead or inhibit other participants; group feeling might block unusual view-points; and the all-too-common research problem that the staged nature of the discussion might 'hot-house' the subject in a way that is disproportionate to its real-life importance.

Depth interview

This is less structured, but more intensive, than an interview using a questionnaire, and varies from allowing any reason-ably relevant response to a semi-structured interview where the interviewer is required to cover a specific list of points. The depth interview avoids the disadvantages of the group dis-cussion and can obtain information from consumers who, for reasons of shyness, inhibition or occupation, are unwilling or unable to attend a group discussion.

Depth interviews are useful for researching individuals' perception of advertisements as, in groups, there is the danger of a dominant member giving an immediate interpretation which is adopted and agreed to by more timorous members.

It is also useful if the subject matter is highly personal, for example personal hygeine or finances, or where there are strongly held social norms which would inhibit open dis-cussion in a group. Lastly, depth interviews are necessary when an understanding is required of complex motivational influences on purchase decision-making. However, the depth interview obviously lacks the dynamics of the group dis-cussion, and is more costly in terms of fieldwork and analysis.

'Kelly' and repertory grid

This is used to investigate respondents' attitudes towards in-dividual brands, products and models. The product field is rep-resented by names on cards, photographs or the packs themselves. First, the respondent is asked to discard any of which he is unaware. He is then presented with randomly se-lected triads (groups of three) by the interviewer, who asks the respondent to specify one way in which two are the same but different from the third. For example, Daz and Omo might be put together as detergents with Dreft as soap powder; or, more usefully, they might be put together as different from another detergent in that they are both more effective in the washing of clothes. The process is repeated using all the brands until the respondent is no longer able to think of any reason why two items are different from a third.

Elicitation interviews
These use open-ended questions such as 'When you go out to buy a (shampoo), what things help you to decide which brand?' or 'How would you describe (brand) to a friend who knew nothing about it?' By repeated probing, salient attributes of products and brands can be elicited.

Projective techniques
This is the use of vague, ambiguous unstructured stimuli to elicit respondents' attitudes and behaviour. They are used to overcome research problems caused by consumers inability or unwillingness to discuss topics. Some examples of this technique have been borrowed direct from psychology:

(a) word association
(b) sentence completion – 'Women who wash their hair every day are . . .'
(c) picture interpretation – the Thematic Apperception Test.

Other techniques have been devised specifically for marketing.

(a) *The 'friendly Martian'*: 'Suppose a Martian had just landed and wanted to buy a car, which one do you think he would choose and why?'
(b) *The 'physical transformation technique'*: 'If a jar of Nescafé coffee came to life, what sort of person do you think it would be?'

4. Summary
The purpose of qualitative research is to obtain information not available by other research methods. While it does not quantify its results, it does provide much of the exploratory and other information on which most quantitative studies are based.

---

1. Introduction
Planning and implementing an advertising campaign requires decision-making on objectives, the size of the budget, the

media and timing of advertising, and the design of the advertisements.

Design of the advertisements comprises three distinct elements.

(a) *Advertising objectives*: The outcome that the campaign is intended to achieve, specified in terms of the intended effect on the target market, e.g. changed attitudes, increased brand loyalty. To allow the effectiveness of the campaign to be assessed, these objectives must be stated in explicit and quantified terms, e.g. '50% increase in brand loyalty among ABC_1 female users within 12 months'.

(b) *Creative strategy*: The concept or theme of the advertising.

(c) *Creative tactics*: The way that the creative strategy is expressed, or 'executed' in the finished advertisements.

Advertising research is involved in the development and assessment of advertisements before publication (pretesting), the assessment of advertisements after publication (posttesting), and in the assessment of advertising media.

2. Advertising Objectives

Advertising objectives derive from the company's marketing objectives and its knowledge of the market. On the basis of panel data (retail and consumer) and possibly a User and Attitudes study, the company might know that the instant coffee market has very few brands, low brand loyalty and high private label penetration. Buyers might be segmented into those who buy only private label and those who switch between branded and private label. A major attitude among consumers might be that branded coffees are all very similar and, whilst superior to private label, are not necessarily worth the additional cost. It might be decided, therefore, to set the advertising objectives of increasing loyalty among buyers of advertised brands and attracting private-label buyers. The target market might be described in SAGACITY[1] terms as 'female, ABC_1 Family, Better off.'

3. Creative Strategy

This follows from the advertising objectives set and from qualitative research, such as group discussions, depth interviews,

---

1. For a full discussion of SAGACITY, see answer to question 16.

and projective tests. It is likely that such research would be conducted specifically for the advertising campaign to amplify the company's existing knowledge of consumer attitudes about instant coffee and to indicate which attitudes to emphasise. Because of consumer inability to discriminate between what are perceived as homogeneous brands, it might be decided that the creative strategy should be to establish the brand as different from other advertised instant coffees and therefore so superior to private labels that the extra cost is insignificant.

This proposed creative strategy can be researched by presenting the proposed concept(s) to samples of the target audience. However, some researchers doubt the usefulness of such research on the grounds that it is impossible to communicate the nature of the concept in a mere verbal description or in a pictorial version that is not so costly as to be prohibitive. (A 30-second TV commercial can cost £100,000 to make.) Therefore, it is said, consumer responses are necessarily so limited that they are of little use in determining the acceptability of the creative idea.

4. Creative Tactics
Research is necessary to assess alternative 'executions' or 'treatments' of the creative strategy. The distinct and quality image of the coffee can be executed in numerous ways, such as:
(a) Using a famous presenter known for his style and taste
(b) Showing the coffee in use in a luxurious setting
(c) Describing how only the best beans are used
(d) Demonstrating the unique roasting process used
At this stage research is used to assess the treatments' success at communicating the creative strategy (*not* assessing the creative strategy itself, which has already been decided.) For example, with the celebrity presenter treatment, it is necessary to research whether he is appropriate – not so elevated that he is incredible, nor so ordinary that the brand is not enhanced; nor too modern, nor too old-fashioned.

Group discussions and/or depth interviews are normally used for this research.

5. Advertising Research Techniques
Assuming that the instant coffee is to be advertised on tele-

vision and in the press, the techniques most likely to be used are as follows.

Television

Advertisements can be tested in various ways. A comparatively inexpensive test that can be used at an early stage involves showing 'animatics' to samples of the target audience. An animatic, or filmed story-board, is a video film made up of stills with a sound track of music, actors' voices. voice-overs, etc., and has the obvious advantage of low sunk cost if it is decided to scrap or fundamentally alter the advertisement. At a later stage in the production, the same test can be done using a finished commercial. Whilst this involves a much greater investment, the use of a finished advertisement is clearly more realistic.

In both cases the advertisement can be shown in a theatre or large hall, a room at a studio or agency, or in a private house. Respondents are asked not whether they think the advertisement is good or bad, but what they understand from it, its associations, the type of people it features and the type of people who they think would use the product. The research is often qualitative, or at least contains open-ended questions to pick up unanticipated reactions.

Press

Advertisements can be tested by including the test advertisement(s) in a folder of other advertisements, all in a similar stage of finish (again depending on the decided trade-off between cost and realism). An alternative and possibly more realistic version of the test is to show the advertisement as part of a specially-prepared magazine or newspaper. In both cases, after a respondent from the target market has had sufficient reading time, he or she is asked questions about which advertisements are remembered, what they contained, associations and so on. The respondent is then shown the advertisement again and asked to comment in more detail. It would also be possible to test press advertisements by *coupon response* – the number of coupons returned or redeemed from different advertisements placed in local or restricted national media. The use of coupons in general has lost favour recently and in any case may not be appropriate to a campaign whose objective is to create quality associations for the product.

Laboratory methods

Both press and television advertisements can be tested by laboratory methods such as psychogalvanometer, eye-blink rate and pupil-dilation. There is much dispute about the usefulness of such methods, since there are great problems in translating the physiological responses into marketing action and consequently such techniques are not widely used. One laboratory method that is used, although mainly for pack and poster testing, is the tachistoscope, although again this is probably inappropriate for the coffee-advertising campaign.

6. Conclusions and Assessment of Pretesting Techniques

Advertising research is one of the most controversial aspects of market research and every technique has its critics. In general, it is claimed that pretesting is:

(a) *Artificial* in respect of the test environment and the semi-finished quality of the advertisements used.

(b) *An innaccurate representation* of the advertising process as, in reality, consumers are much less aware of advertising. Advertisements communicate and influence in a cumulative manner over time, rather than the single exposure, immediate context of the tests.

However, some assessment is essential when very large sums of money are being committed and can be a useful aid to decision-making if its possibilities and limitations are realised. Whilst research on its own will not develop the best advertising strategy or tactics, it can indicate fruitful directions and screen out potential mistakes. At the execution stage it will not show *how* successful the advertising will be. It can determine whether it is meeting the objectives set in terms of communicating clearly, establishing the required associations and imagery and avoiding undesired effects.

Answer 24   **Test Marketing**   Question page 5

---

1. The Nature of Test Marketing

A test market is a national marketing plan that is tested

locally to observe and monitor its results, principally sales. While test marketing is often thought of only in terms of the experimental launch of a new product, it includes also the testing of variations to one or more parts of the marketing mix, for example a new pack design or a price reduction. The purpose is to 'try out' the proposed marketing plan in the relatively low cost of a local market rather than, and prior to, a wider or national launch.

In some countries, notably the United States, often a number of areas are used to pretest a range of alternative marketing strategies, for example different advertising themes or budgets or different prices. In the UK, mainly because of the size and cost of the size and cost of the available ITV areas and the national structure of much of the press, the practice is to pretest one strategy in one area.

Test marketing allows the entire marketing plan to be analysed in a real setting. Rather than asking questions about intentions and attitudes, it is possible to observe actual consumer behaviour in the market place. On the basis of test market results, decisions can be made to extend the plan.

To be a valid indicator of national performance, the test market must meet the following criteria:

(a) The test area must be representative of the national market, in terms of relevant consumers, distribution and media.

(b) The level of marketing activity must be proportionate to the test area's size in relation to the national market. It is essential to avoid the tendency to 'hot-house', i.e. the over-concentration of effort in the test area in a way that will not be replicated at national level.

(c) The length of the test must be sufficient to demonstrate the established repeat buying pattern and any seasonal influences.

(d) It must be possible to measure the results, particularly consumer purchase.

2. Criticisms of Test Marketing
Several major criticisms are made of test marketing. First, it is expensive, especially in the UK, if television is involved, because of the relatively large size of the television areas. Sec-

ond, there is an opportunity cost in the delay caused to the marketing plan. A third criticism concerns the information that it allows competitors to gather about the company's new product and marketing plan.

Fourth, it is claimed that none of the available test areas is representative of the national market. Last, test marketing has been criticised for not predicting national results; it is said that it is impossible to isolate or measure the effects of extraneous factors, such as freak weather or industrial disputes, and that in any case test marketing takes so long that by the time the results can be applied market conditions have inevitably changed.

3. Test Marketing a New Brand of Fruit Juice
As a result of research in product development and testing, advertising and pricing, the company will have arrived at a marketing plan. This should be translated into objectives for sales, market penetration, adoption and repeat purchase; it is these objectives that are to be tested. The company might also be seeking information on distribution, such as the performance of the product and pack.

Need for a test market
Any test market is bound to be expensive, and the company should consider 'mini-testing'. Whilst this does not create completely the market conditions of a full test, it does offer many of the characteristics at a greatly reduced cost. The major form of 'mini-test' in the UK is the use of a panel of housewives who are visited each week by a mobile shop, from which they make purchases of a range of foods and household products. By calling on the same housewives regularly and over time, information on trial and repurchase can be obtained at relatively low cost. Whilst these results might not be considered adequate to provide a forecast for national sales, they do indicate whether the project is worth proceeding with and/or whether more extensive testing is required.

This type of testing would be quite appropriate for a fruit juice.

Area in which to test
Assuming that it is decided that a full test market is necessary, the first decision is to select the area. If it is proposed to use television as a major advertising medium, this means

selecting between television areas. Border and South West have the advantage of small size (and, therefore relatively low cost) but might be considered unrepresentative of the UK as a whole because of geographical remoteness, low population and climate.

The areas often used are Lancashire, South of England and Anglia, and the choice should be made on the basis of representation of the target market for the product, (in terms of demography and consumption patterns) target distribution outlets and cost.

Duration of test market

The objective of the test market is to establish conditions as similar as possible to those that will affect the product when on sale in the national market and thereby to assess its chances of success, using a similar marketing strategy. It is necessary, therefore, to ascertain not only the initial trial rate but also the adoption and repurchase levels. The sales level that can be expected for the product nationally will be calculated on the basis of regular buyers multiplied by their purchase rate.

Therefore, sufficient time must be allowed for regular buying patterns to settle down. The length required for this varies, and test markets last anything from 2 to 24 months. In the case of the fruit juice, there are bound to be seasonal and climatic influences, with sales peaking in summer, particularly if the weather is hot. While the test market cannot last long enough to take account of good and bad summers, it should cover the seasons in which it is intended to sell the product.

It is not essential for the test to last for an entire year, provided that the plan is to sell only during the summer, or to sell the product throughout the year and for summer sales to be a sufficient target with any winter sales as a bonus.

Further, if the company has considerable experience in the product field, it might feel confident enough to reduce the test period. However, extensive research by Nielsen shows that test markets of 6 months or less are only two-thirds as likely adequately to predict market share as those lasting 8 months or more.

Data to be collected

The objective of conducting the test market is to collect data on the marketing plan's performance. The analysis of this data is the final stage of the test. However, decisions must be made in advance on the data required and the means to be used for collection.

Ex-factory or ex-warehouse sales are usually easily available, but give very little indication of consumer buying. Therefore, the company must ensure that retail and home audit sales data are available, from either syndicated sources or its own tailor-made surveys. In addition to sales data, the company should use the test market to examine the behaviour of other marketing variables, for example the enthusiasm of its salesforce, the reaction of the trade, the success of any point-of-sale material and the performance of packaging. Lastly, a consumer research study among buyers during the test period is of value in providing data on post-purchase satisfaction.

4. Summary
Test marketing is a unique way of pretesting marketing plans. It is expensive, but can provide a wide range of information about performace in actual market conditions.

Answer 25   **Industrial Market Research**   Question page 6

---

1. Industrial Marketing[1]
In order to examine industrial market research, it is first necessary to consider industrial marketing, and to appreciate that the term includes a range of market types:

(a) *Producer/manufacturer markets*: Companies and organisations in the public and private sectors who buy (or rent) goods and services to be used in the production of other goods and services; for example, an engineering company buying machine tools, or a transport company buying trucks or buses.

(b) *Re-seller markets*: Retailers, wholesalers and agents, buying for resale.

(c) *Government market*: Government departments (at national and local levels) buying (or renting) the goods and services

1. For a full discussion of industrial marketing, see answer to question 46.

required for carrying out the function of government; for example, the Education Department buying books and schools, and the Defence Department buying missiles and fighter planes.

The common thread through all these market types is a small number of customers (relative to most consumer markets) within each of which buying is usually done by groups called Decision Making Units (DMUs) using mainly rational criteria.

2. Market Research[2]

Market research is the collection, analysis and interpretation of information about consumers, products, competitors and other environmental factors, with the purpose of providing guidance and risk-reduction in the taking of marketing decisions.

In all market research exercises, there are certain stages to the research process:

(a) problem definition
(b) research design
(c) data collection
(d) data analysis
(e) report presentation

This much is equally applicable to both industrial and consumer market research.

3. Industrial and Consumer Market Research

There are three major differences between industrial and consumer market research.

The populations or universes studied

Consumer markets tend to be made up of very large numbers of fairly similar people, with similar buying needs and habits. Consider, for example, housewives buying breakfast cereals, detergents or frozen vegetables. Industrial markets, on the contrary, are usually much smaller with more varied buyers. For example, ball-bearing purchasers are limited to specialized engineering companies and can vary between a very large motor vehicle producer and a small company making roller skates.

2. For a full discussion of the scope of market research see answer to question 17.

Data sought

Consumer market research data are both quantitative – market size and shares, and qualitative – consumer attitudes, motivations and lifestyle. Industrial market research, is almost entirely concerned with quantitative data. Further, research is used much more extensively in consumer markets. First, there is more research done (in relation to sales) and, second, this research includes topics very rarely formally investigated by industrial research; for example, the continuous monitoring of sources of purchase (Nielsen), and the effect on sales of promotions.

Methods of data collection

Because of these differences in populations and data there are differences in the methods used for data collection. Consumer research uses techniques such as group discussions, depth interviews and projective tests to obtain qualitative data; it also uses large samples to collect quantitative data on usage and attitude studies and for continuous research panels; it uses observational studies and, for product evaluation, hall and placement tests. Industrial research concentrates much more on the desk research of secondary data, questionnaires to small samples and the expert opinion of users and specialists.

4. The Tasks of Industrial Market Research

Industrial market research is concerned with providing general information on markets and the potential for particular companies within markets.

General information related to markets

Market size: Total market size by volume (tonnage, square footage, gallonage, units etc.) and value; factors limiting market size, e.g. legal restrictions, government policies, new technology.

Market structure: Market shares of main suppliers, split between domestic and foreign suppliers; market segments by user-size, industry, product characteristics such as price, quantity, design, specification.

Buying methods: Central/localised influence; types of DMUs; buying cycles, e.g. government financial years; types of tenders and estimates required.

Market trends: Seasonal and cyclical variations; long

term trends, e.g. comparison of present market size with previous 5, 10 years and projection for next 1, 5, 10 years; projected changes in requirements in terms of product type, design, price, specification, e.g. lightweight components for cars; current and projected changes in user and non-user industries related to demand, e.g. computerisation of cash tills; other environmental factors to which demand is sensitive, levels of income, employment and production, consumer expenditure, taxation, credit, inflation, balance of payments, demography, social changes, government and politics.

Buyer/market requirements: A segmentational analysis of market requirements in terms of product specification, price, delivery, service, guarantees, credit, technical advice, ideal product.

Channels of distribution: Structure of distribution in the market, e.g. direct, retailers wholesalers, agents; costs and trends, e.g. in food retailing, the move to superstores and electronic stock control; relationship between suppliers and distributors, e.g. assistance given to distributors; effectiveness of distributors' selling methods; arrangements on exclusive dealing, franchising, maintenance, servicing; levels of stock carried; policies on discounts and SOR (sale or return).

Physical distribution: Costs, speed and methods; allocation of distributive tasks between channel members, e.g. are manufacturers expected to undertake transport, storage?; pack sizes used; requirements in terms of handling, climate, shelf life.

Selling and promotional methods: Selling methods used, sizes of sales forces, (type of salesmen used, in terms of technical knowledge and education) use of wholesaler sales forces and agents; aids required by salesmen, such as catalogues, samples, demonstrations, technical advice; levels of advertising expenditure and media used; use of exhibitions and direct mail.

Competition: Major competitors by products sold, present and trend market shares; competitors' strengths and weaknesses; competitive products by quality, durability, technical specification, performance, design, finish, durability, depth and width of ranges; distribution, service, guarantees offered; manufacturing potential, technical and research abilities and resources; quality of management and personnel.

5. The Status and Potential of Competitors

This derives from comparing the company with competitors, in terms of reputation, image, products, R and D, sales and distribution, service and technical back-up. Such analysis indicates strengths, necessary improvements and favourable areas for activity and expansion. For example, a packaging company might compare with competitors as offering high quality but at high prices, technologically advanced in the growing plastic materials segment, but with a small share of the stable but large corrugated cardboard segment.

6. Data Collection Methods

Industrial market research relies heavily on desk research – the use of secondary or existing information. A major source of such information for industrial research is government statistics. The Government Statistical Office issues an annual booklet listing publications available. In addition to the basic Monthly Digest of Statistics and the Annual Abstract of Statistics, there are Business Monitors for various industries, the National Food Survey, the General Household Survey, the Family Expenditure Survey, Department of Employment Gazette, National Income and Expenditure Blue Book, import/export publications and so on. These publications can either be purchased, or referred to at the Market Intelligence library in London.

A further official source of data is Companies' House, where there is financial information, for example sales and profits of companies; such information can be useful when estimating market sizes and shares.

Trade associations such as the SMMT (Society of Motor Manufacturers and Traders) often compile very detailed information on market sizes, shares, development and trends.

Estimates and forecasts of market size and potential are often based on product-related data obtained by desk research. For example, estimates for a lens-grinding machine might be based on a factor of the number of companies producing and processing lenses.

Original or primary industrial market research data are usually collected by questionnaires. Often, the sample size is small, i.e. 10–20 respondents representing buyers. Questionnaires tend to be long and administered by personal interview, with numerous open-ended questions. Telephone interviewing is also used extensively with postal surveys for large samples. In all cases it is essential to locate those people within organisations who are influential in the buying decision.

Product testing consists of evaluating functional attributes and the opinion of engineers and other key users is of major importance.

7. Conclusion
While industrial market research is important in marketing decision making, its scope is much more limited in terms of both data sought and data collection methods than consumer market research.

Answer 26   **Brief description of ...**   Question page 6

(a) BARB
(b) JICNARS
(c) JICRARS
(d) Hall tests
(e) Placement tests
(f) Omnibus studies
(g) *Ad hoc* research
(h) Observation Studies
(i) Clinical research.

(a) BARB
BARB – Broadcasters' Audience Research Board, produces estimates of television audiences sizes for BBC1, BBC2, ITV and Channel 4 programmes. BARB represents the BBC and the ITV companies and users of ITV advertising. (Before BARB was established in 1981, BBC and ITV audiences were measured separately, ITV by JICTAR). The audience measurement is carried out by the research company AGB (Audits of Great Britain) using a quota sample of 2900 households, (nearly 8000 individuals) throughout the United Kingdom and representing each of the ITV regions. In each household, a meter attached to the television set (and, where appropriate, to a

second set) records when the set is switched on and the station to which it is tuned. As the meter cannot account for the number of people (if any) present, each member of the household completes a diary indicating at which times (s)he was viewing.

Data on viewing figures are published weekly and are broken down by ITV region, socio-economic group, sex, age, and so on, and form the basis for the advertising rates charged and for all media planning involving television.

(b) JICNARS

JICNARS – the Joint Industry Committee for National Readership Surveys – produces estimates of the readership of over 100 newspapers and magazines throughout the United Kingdom. The Joint Industry Committee represents both media owners and users. While data are available on the circulation, or numbers sold, media planners need to know the numbers and types of readers.

The National Readership Survey's (NRS) objective is to provide information that is necessary for the assessment and efficient use of media and which is acceptable to both publishers and buyers of space in the media concerned. The Survey is conducted among individuals aged fifteen and over using a randomly-selected annual sample of 30,000, interviewed through the year at a rate of 600 a week.

Data collection is by personal interview in the homes of respondents, using a 'Masthead' booklet to aid recall and minimise confusion between 'titles'. The 'Masthead' booklet contains reproductions of the logos of the newspaper and magazines concerned. The NRS measures the frequency with which individuals 'read or look at' publications and also the average issue readership. Respondents are classified by a range of variables, for example socio-economic grade, sex, age, employment status, ownership and recent acquisition of various consumer durables and moving house during the past six years.

(c) JICRAR

JICRAR – the Joint Industry Committee for Radio Audience Research – produces estimates of the size of radio audiences in the UK. (Although BBC and Radio Luxembourg figures are included, these two companies produce separate estimates of their audiences.) JICRAR uses random samples of 800–1,000 individuals in each IBA radio area, who complete diaries recording their listening quarter-hour by quarter-hour. These diaries are necessarily self-completed, but are placed and collected by interviewers, and distinguish between listening 'at home' and 'elsewhere'. As the research is expensive, it is carried out only once a year (in contrast to the continuous panel used for television), with the interviewing and diary-keeping spread over four weeks.

Both BBC and Luxembourg research their audiences by use of '24-hour recall', whereby a quota sample is asked by street interview for details of listening during the previous day, with recall aided by means of programme cards.

(d) Hall tests

Hall tests are a means of collecting research data by bringing a sample of the target group into a hall or theatre, and are used for research exercises that are too complex or protracted for street interviewing. For example, a hall test might be used in the pretesting of advertisements, using folder tests or animatics. Respondents can be shown a number of proposed advertising treatments or executions, in a fairly relaxed and leisurely atmosphere, and questioned on the relative communication effects and associations.

Similarly, a hall test provides a suitable environment for product testing; respondents can be asked to taste food and drink products, consider colours and designs for carpets, wall-tiles or packaging and answer questions on preference, ranking, product features, likelihood of purchasing and so on.

Hall tests are conducted in areas, and at times, appropriate to attract members of the target group who are usually recruited by quota sample, possibly with some small reward for participation, such as some confectionery or an inexpensive pen.

(e) Placement tests

Product usage often involves many stages that are important to the purchase decision. For example, whereas a hall test could be used to research a new packet soup's attributes in terms of taste, texture and visual impact, the setting is inappropriate for the research of consumer attitudes and behaviour in respect of preparation and the response of the entire family. Placement tests operate by giving samples of the product to members of the target group for consumption at home. After use, respondents are interviewed on their experience and response on topics such as convenience of the pack, convenience in preparation and attitude of other family members.

Placement tests are useful also in obtaining information on consumer durables, such as washing machines and cameras, and can assist in product design.

(f) Omnibus surveys

Omnibus surveys are carried out by research companies who draw the samples, administer the questionnaires, process the data and report results. Client companies can purchase 'space' on the questionnaire and pay according to the number and type of questions asked, (open-ended cost more than precoded) and the statistical breakdown required. The number of questions that an individual client can include is limited, but in some cases can be sufficient to obtain the data required, especially as in addition to general omnibus surveys there are specialist versions for markets such as motoring and baby products and new home owners. An omnibus study can be a quick and inexpensive means of obtaining simple, yet important data; for example, the frequency with which individuals clean their cars, and the proportion of consumers planning an overseas holiday. There is, however, the disadvantage that a shared questionnaire is likely to range over a number of subjects so that it is difficult to engage respondents' attention in more than a superficial way. Although this does not apply quite so much to a specialist omnibus, the questionnaire still represents the interests of a number of sponsors.

(g) *Ad hoc* Research

Ad hoc is defined as 'arranged for this purpose', and in market research means a single study of a problem. Such a study can be of quite long duration, such as a test market, or as brief as a single group discussion. *Ad hoc* research takes a 'snapshot' of a market and provides a description and analysis of particular market conditions at a particular time. It can be contrasted with continuous research, such as retail auditing or advertising campaign tracking, which provides longitudinal trend data showing the development of market conditions over time.

(h) Observation Studies

Observation techniques developed from anthropological studies of customs and behaviour. In market research typically it consists of an investigator watching some simple household process to find possibilities for product improvement and development. Direct observation of what people *do* rather than what they *say* they do can give data of increased accuracy, as there is no dependence on consumer honesty and memory. Observation studies are used to investigate problems such as: what processes does a housewife follow when cleaning floors, what tools does she use, does she scrub, wash, polish; what stage presents the most difficulty? And, therefore, would a combined cleaner and polish or a self-shine polish be an advantage?

Other forms of observation study are the AGB Television Consumer Audit, where investigators inspect household stocks and used packs; and point-of-purchase observation to study behaviour when buying – do consumers pick up the first pack they see, do they compare prices, do they search for a particular brand?

The main disadvantage of an observation study is the high cost of fieldwork because of the time taken, the need for skilled investigators and the problems of coding the results. In addition, it should be noted that observation studies report only *what* happened and give no indication of the *reasons* for behaviour.

(i) Clinical research

Clinical or laboratory research is a mechanical means of observation using techniques borrowed directly from psychological research. Rather than *asking* consumers how they react to or feel about products, advertisements, packs, etc., clinical research seeks to measure consumer reactions objectively.

It is true to say that such techniques are part of the history of marketing fads and, with very few exceptions, have been found to have only limited application to the solution of market research problems. The clinical techniques tried in market research are: the psychogalvanometer, or 'lie-detector' to measure arousal and response to advertisements; cameras to measure pupil dilation (and thereby interest) in response to advertisements; cameras to measure eye movement (and thereby interest) over advertisements; cameras to measure eye-blink rate (and thereby 'state of mind') in response to advertisements and more particularly in supermarkets; and the tachistoscope to measure the length of time necessary to read a headline or recognise a pack.

All these techniques have been found to be expensive, cumbersome and artificial in use and, with the exception of the tachistoscope, provide data that are too vague to be informative.

It should be noted that strictly, the set meter used in the measurement of television audiences is a clinical technique, although it does measure behaviour rather than the physiological changes that might precede or are associated with behaviour.

Answer 27　　　**Product Life Cycle**　　　Question page 6

---

1. The Product Life Cycle in Theory

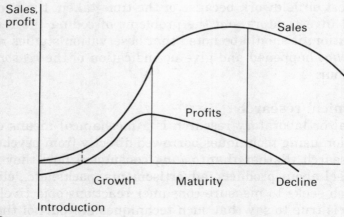

Fig. 10

The Product Life Cycle (PLC) is a theoretical description of the sales of a product over time, invariably divided into four stages: Introduction, Growth, Maturity and Decline.

(a) *Introduction*: Slow growth of sales, as the product is introduced to the market, and no profit because of low revenue and the high expenses of establishing the product.

(b) *Growth*: Rapid market acceptance and improvement in profit level.

(c) *Maturity*: Stabilisation of sales because the product is accepted by all, or most, potential buyers; decreasing profits caused by need to defend market share against competition.

(d) *Decline*: Both sales and profit fall.

2. The Product Life Cycle in Practice

The PLC is an attempt to generalise for all products and consequently, as a guide for marketing decision-making, it can be criticised in the following ways.

(a) It gives no time-scales or sales levels.

(b) It does not distinguish between types of product, between product types and brands or between continuous and discontinuous innovations.[1]

(c) Comparing PLC theory with the empirical sales data of a range of brands, some writers have even concluded that in practice PLC does not exist.

(d) The most significant criticism of PLC for marketing practitioners is that the cycle is not inevitable, but can be modified by marketing activity.

3. Modifying the Product Life Cycle

Introduction

The theoretical slow sales growth can be accelerated by a penetration strategy of low price and/or high promotional expenditures with extensive distribution. Using a strategy of this type, the Introduction stage for a *continuous* innovation, aimed at a large, price-sensitive market, could be shortened and the brand established in the market quickly, with consequent advantages over completion.

Growth

Again, this can be accelerated in many cases by the use of aggressive marketing and promotion.

1. For a discussion of continuous and discontinuous innovations, see answer to question 13.

Maturity

Sales levels can be raised by increasing market penetration, i.e. attracting more users, and/or increasing the usage rate of the product among existing users. For example, a manufacturer of a brand of muesli could seek to attract users of other muesli brands or other types of breakfast cereal; alternatively, the company could persuade existing users that they should eat more muesli by increasing the size of their portions, by eating it on occasions other than breakfast or by using it as a cooking ingredient.

There are various strategies available to achieve these objectives, the selection of which depends on prevailing market factors. For example, the brand could be 'relaunched' with a price cut, heavy promotion and/or product improvement. However, unless this relaunch does involve some product improvement as perceived by buyers, it is likely that any increase in sales will last only as long as the promotion or price reduction. A more enduring effect can be achieved by using the relaunch to 'reposition' the product in the market, now suitable for new or more frequent use, as described above. The most radical strategy is actually to modify the product by offering it in changed or additional forms. For example, new products could be developed, such as muesli bars or muesli yoghurt.

Decline

The future pattern of sales at this stage is uncertain, and depends on the underlying cause of the decline. First, if like the radio valve the product has been superseded by technology, or like flaired trousers has gone out of fashion, the only strategy is that of 'divest' or immediate discontinuation. Second, if sales have declined to a lower but stable level, a 'hold' strategy of reduced promotion might well succeed in maintaining a reduced but profitable level of sales. Third, if sales have reduced to a very low level, it might be profitable to use a 'harvesting' or 'milking' strategy of ceasing all marketing expenditures while still maintaining distribution of the product.

However, declining sales can be reversed by appropriate and intense marketing activity. In a famous Harvard Business Review article, Yuspeh and Dhalla point out that if PLC is accepted without analysis of the underlying causes, it can become a self-fulfilling prophecy so that the decline in sales is brought about as much by marketing activity (or inactivity) as by inevitable market or environmental factors. It is necessary, therefore, to assess the causes of decline and, if appropriate, invest marketing resources in one of the positive strategies described for the Maturity stage.

4. Conclusion
The PLC has been criticised for being a generalisation for all products and therefore accurate for none. Its greatest value for marketing management is in the analysis of the direction of a product's sales and of the underlying reasons for this direction. Using this information, it is possible to develop strategies to modify the PLC to the advantage of the company.

Question 28   **The New Product**   Question page 6
                     Development Process

---

1. The New Product Development Process
The new product development process is a representation of the entire Marketing Concept – the generation, development, promotion and distribution of market-oriented innovations, and is a vital element therefore of every company's activity. Notwithstanding criticism of traditional Product Life Cycle Theory,[1] a company must develop new products in order to grow.

A 'new product' can be defined as varying from: *a completely new product*, such as the Kodak disc camera; *an improved product*, such as an existing model of a camera to which a built-in flash has been added; *a product modification*, such as an existing camera with a redesigned shape; or a new version of an existing product type, such as a new brand of single-lens reflex camera.

The stages through which a new product is developed are:
(a) idea generation
(b) screening and testing
(c) business analysis
(d) product development

1. For a full discussion of Product Life Cycle Theory, see answer 27.

105

(e) test marketing

(f) launch or commercialisation.

2. Idea Generation

Ideas for new products can come from sources internal or external to the company and be market-oriented or laboratory-oriented. Internal sources include employees in general, salespeople and specifically established departments, such as Market Research and New Product Development; the use of data from market segmentation studies, and from scientific or laboratory research which can produce technologically feasible new product ideas. External sources include the complaints and comments of customers and dealers and, more often, the innovations of competitors. Many so-called 'new products' are very similar 'me-too' versions of recently introduced products, and this strategy is likely to be successful only when demand for a product exceeds supply. Other external sources include inventors, commercial laboratories and market research and advertising agencies.

3. Screening and Testing

Having developed a new product idea, for example a mild shampoo in gel form with stripes that contain an anti-dandruff agent, it is necessary to decide whether it is a 'good' idea.

The concept of the product must be tested on potential buyers to investigate whether they perceive it as comprehensible and credible and as a sufficient improvement on existing products to justify purchase. Consumers might consider the product a novelty, but with no relevance to their needs. However, even a product that is attractive to consumers might not be attractive to the company. The company must examine the technological and production feasibility, whether the likely range of cost and revenue structures will yield a profit, and the product's compatibility with company objectives, image, product range and distribution.

4. Business Analysis

The concept testing and screening stage represents a feasibility study to establish the product idea's general viability. Before committing the extensive investment required to develop the product, it is necessary to estimate fairly accurately the projected cash flow. These figures, derived from estimates of costs – developmental, production and marketing – and of revenue, play a major part in the decision to develop the product further.

It should be noted that expectation of 'profit' is not sufficient basis for proceeding with the product. It is necessary to quantify this profit in terms of *Return on Capital* invested and the length of time before it is received, and to compare the resultant 'Pay-back' figures with the potential profits from alternative investment opportunities available to the company.

5. Product Development

Provided that the product idea meets the criteria set under Business Analysis, it passes to the Product Development stage. Product Development has two functions; first, to convert the product idea into a physical form, and second to develop a basic marketing strategy. This stage sees a great increase in expenditure as a physical version of the product idea is developed and tested in terms of both product performance and consumer attitudes.

The company's Research and Development department seeks to develop a prototype which meets the following criteria.

(a) Is perceived by consumers as embodying the key attributes of the product concept.

(b) Performs safely under normal use conditions.

(c) Is capable of production within the budgeted costs.

The costs and time required at this development stage depend on the product's characteristics. For example, a highly technical industrial product such as a machine tool requires a long period of expensive technological development, whereas a toiletry product such as anti-dandruff shampoo involves much less concentration in these areas, but much more attention to consumer research and product positioning.

A number of the finished prototype are tested *functionally* in laboratory or field conditions to investigate factors such as (in the shampoo example) effectiveness at treating dandruff, other effects on hair condition, ease of rinsing, strength of packaging and so on. *Attitude* tests investigate how consumers feel about attributes of the product; for example, does the pack design, product colour and smell give the impression that it will be effective against dandruff, while being mild.

6. Test Marketing[2]

Having developed the product, it is necessary to design a complete marketing plan, involving the advertising campaign, distribution and price. Whilst all these Marketing Mix variables can (and should) be researched in ways similar to those used in product development, it is highly desirable to 'try out' the Marketing Plan without the huge financial risk involved with a national launch.

Therefore, to assess its effectiveness, the Marketing Plan is tested in a local market that is representative of the national market. Test Marketing allows the entire Marketing Plan to be analysed in a real setting. Rather than *asking questions* about consumer intentions and attitudes it is possible to *observe consumer behaviour* in the market place in response to the proposed marketing activity.

It is essential that the Test Market lasts long enough for buying patterns to become established and for any seasonal effects to be observed.

7. Commercialisation and Launch

The decision on whether or not to launch the product to the full target market involves the greatest cost of the product development process. Deciding to go ahead requires investment in manufacturing plant and equipment, advertising, promotion and possibly an extended sales force. Deciding on the basis of the test market results *not* to go ahead involves little or no additional expenditure, but requires abandoning the investment made to date. Accountants emphasise the fact that heavy past expenditure or 'sunk cost' is not a logical reason for further expenditure, but human nature often makes this advice difficult to accept and it is essential to overlook all feelings of sentiment and commitment to irretrievable investment.

The decision to launch implies consequent decisions. First, *when* to launch in order to benefit form any seasonal factors or to anticipate possible competitive activity. Second, *where* to launch, i.e. either a complete national launch or a

2. For a full discussion of Test Marketing, see answer 24.

'roll-out' strategy with phased increases in production facilities and marketing expenditure.

8. Product Development from Outside Sources

While the focus of New Product Development is often on the entire process occurring within the company, many of the stages can take place elsewhere, with the company developing product ideas or even products that originate from outside sources. Thus, the company might buy and develop product ideas or commercialise finished products which others have developed but been unable to progress for lack of funds or expertise.

Product development is also possible by acquiring the rights to manufacture or distribute in the domestic market the products of an overseas company; or by taking over a product already on sale but the full potential of which has not been realised because of poor marketing.

9. Conclusion

Innovation is essential to growth and involves complexity and a high level of risk. The probability of successful innovation can be maximised, and the level of risk minimised, by following a process of new product development that not only produces new ideas, but also assesses and analyses them at various stages before progression to each more expensive further stage.

Answer 29	**Organisational Structure for New Product Development**	Question page 7

---

1. New Product Development

Most companies have growth as a major goal, because history shows that if companies do not grow, they do not stand still – they shrink. New product development, as a major means of growth, is therefore of such central importance that many companies establish organisational structures specifically for the purpose.

New product development is the generation, promotion and distribution of market-oriented innovations and involves the following stages.

(a) Idea generation
(b) Screening and testing
(c) Business analysis
(d) Product development
(e) Test marketing
(f) Launch, or commercialisation.

2. Organisation for New Product Development

Incorporating new product development into the organisational structure gives emphasis and priority not only to the generation and flow of new product ideas but also to the elimination at the earliest possible stage of ideas that are not suitable and the progress and development of ideas that are.

New product development organisation takes the following forms.

(a) Product/Brand Managers
(b) New Product Managers
(c) New Product Committees
(d) New Product Departments
(e) New Product Venture Teams.

Whatever structure is adopted, it is essential to establish an explicit and consistent policy, so that everyone concerned has a clear understanding of the company's growth strategy. Unless this is done, time and money can be wasted on developing products that are subsequently rejected, not because of lack of profit potential, but because they are incompatible with company objectives.

3. Product/Brand Managers[1]

For many reasons this is possibly the least effective organisational structure for new product development. First, most product managers already have enough to do in looking after their own existing products and have a natural tendency to concentrate on these immediate and pressing tasks rather than on the more reflective and speculative activity of innovation. Second, they are not trained in the skills necessary for product development.

1. For a full discussion of the Product/Brand Manager system, see answer 7.

4. New Product Managers

This system is to appoint a manager responsible solely for product development and it has been successful in companies where the post has been given sufficient status and where there is no pressure to produce results. However, there is a danger that the New Product Manager's status is junior, and that he is considered as being in the job because he is not up to being a product manager.

In this case, he does not have the authority to steer new products through the numerous and hazardous stages to launch. Also, there is a tendency (often encouraged by top management) for the New Product Manager to think in terms of product modifications rather than in completely innovative terms.

5. New Product Committees

This is a more elaborate arrangement than the previous two. The Committee is composed of representatives from the major functional areas within the company – not only marketing, but also engineering, production, research and development and finance. Its primary function is to establish a system that will provide a flow of new product ideas, determine which should be further developed and assign the necessary tasks to the appropriate departments.

The New Product Committee system has the advantage that its members usually have sufficient importance within the company to give the committee's decisions the authority necessary to ensure that priority is given to the new product ideas that come forward. Unfortunately, this same importance of committee members also means that they have other demanding responsibilities in their own departments. Consequently, they are likely to be unable to allocate the necessary time to product development and often send deputies or are replaced, so that continuity is lost.

6. New Product Departments

New Product Departments are an attempt to establish a more permanent and dedicated organisational structure. It is a version of the New Product Manager approach expanded to a department headed by a senior executive, reporting direct to the Managing Director. The Department is responsible for the new product development process from idea generation up to and including test market, after which stage the project is handed over to a product manager or company department for national launch.

The system's major disadvantage derives from this hand-over stage, which can result in confusion over location of responsibility for the product. The New Product Department might well consider that its involvement ends once the product manager has taken over, whereas the product manager might have reservations about a marketing plan which he had no part in developing.

7. New Product Venture Teams

This is a group of experts brought together specifically to develop a product. Unlike New Product Departments, they carry the product right through to launch and turn it over to a product manager or department only *after* it has been established in the national market, thus avoiding confusion over responsibility. Despite this improvement, and the advantages of team-spirit and commitment, there is the danger that team members can become so involved in the project that they lose their objectivity, take unnecessary risks and take the product beyond the stage at which it should have been abandoned. This danger can be reduced by the use of predetermined controls and criteria.

8. Product Development Involving External Sources

Whilst the focus of New Product Development is often on the entire process occurring within the company, many of the stages can take place elsewhere. The company can develop product ideas originating from outside sources such as advertising agencies, competitors, customers or inventors. In contrast, the company can acquire developed products by distributing or making under licence products developed by overseas companies in other markets. Another option is to buy the rights to a product which has been produced by another company, which for reasons of inadequate resources, skills or application has not been commercialised to full potential.

A different organisational structure is required for these forms of product development, and usually takes the form of a senior executive charged with discovering and recommending suitable products to the Board of Directors.

9. Conclusion

Whilst it is essential to separate the reflective, creative and analytical process of product development from the more immediate task of managing existing products, there is no single organisational structure that is without fault and suited to every need. Consequently, companies tend to develop the structure that best suits their individual organisation and objectives.

Answer 30   Product Planning   Question page 7

---

1. The Scope of Product Planning

Product planning is the development and management of the company's products. As the range and quality of products offered is a major determinant of the company's success, product planning is of the highest importance. It involves decisions both short and long term, in the following areas.
(a) The mix of products to be offered – the Product Mix.
(b) The evaluation and management of current products.
(c) The development of existing and new products.
(d) The discontinuation of products.
(e) The branding and positioning of products.

2. The Product Mix

The Product Mix is the central factor in product planning. Most companies have more than one product, so product planning requires decision-making not only on individual products but also on the overall product line. At the strategic level, decisions about which markets to enter and the mix of products to offer are fundamental to the company's development and growth.

Products can be classified on the basis of *buyer* or *market* type, such as industrial, consumer, service; or by *product* type, such as durable and f.m.c.g. (fast moving consumer good).

The product mix of a company can be described in terms of width, depth and consistency. *Width* refers to the number of different product lines, e.g. Levi's jeans, jackets, trousers, shirts and shoes. *Depth* refers to the number of items within each product line e.g., Levi's range of styles, colours, sizes, fabrics for jeans, jackets and so on. *Consistency* refers to the relationship between the product lines in terms of end-use, production requirements, distribution channels and marketing skills necessary.

3. The Evaluation and Management of Current Products

No product mix is permanent, and must be reviewed continuously in response to the changing needs and wants of consumers, competitive activity and environmental factors. It is necessary to assess the performance and prospects of current products and allocate marketing support accordingly, using portfolio analysis such as the Boston Box.

4. The Development of Current and New Products

Portfolio analysis will indicate any ways in which the product line requires lengthening by the development or addition of new products. A product line can be lengthened by *filling* or *stretching*.

Line filling involves the introduction of products in between those already offered; for example, Levi cords fill a gap in the product line between Levi denim jeans and Levi hopsack trousers. It is essential to avoid overfilling the product line, as this can lead to cannibalisation, whereby sales of a new product are gained only at the expense of sales of existing products elsewhere in the line.

Line stretching means extending the product line into a new area. It is essential that line stretching does not damage the marketing strategy or image of current products. Thus, Pepsi-Cola researched Diet Pepsi to ensure that its appeal to the weight-conscious would not tarnish its carefree, young image; and Seiko introduced a separate brand, Pulsar, in order to move into the lower-price watch market.

In addition to lengthening the product line the company can decide to change its range by *modernising* products that have become outdated as a result of the passage of time or the introduction by the competition of new products. This is seen particularly in the car industry with frequent replacement models and 'face-lifts'.

A further means of product line development is *line featuring*, or using one or a few items in the line to draw attention and sales to the rest of the line. Major users of this approach are retailers who promote particular products, e.g. low-priced coffee in a supermarket in order to attract customers to the store where, it is hoped, they will then buy their entire weekly shop.

5. The Discontinuation of Products

In addition to developing products in the line and adding new ones, product planning involves *line pruning*, or the dropping of products. A product should be dropped when it is clear that the resources required for its continuation could be employed more profitably elsewhere. In other words a product might be dropped even if it is making a profit, if that profit is less than could be achieved through alternative use of resources.

It is essential to investigate the total costs of retaining a weak product. These include high inventory costs, short (and expensive) production runs and the creation of a bad image for the company and the rest of its products. However, the major cost is that by taking a disproportionate amount of managerial time and energy, weak products can deflect attention from the objective of developing the new products that form the basis of the company's future profits.

Such products fall into two categories. First, those in the Decline stage of the Product Life Cycle (although declining or reduced sales alone are not sufficient reason for dropping a product). In the Decline stage, investment and development costs have long since been written off, and the marketing and promotional expenditure necessary in a 'harvesting' strategy can be quite low, with the result that quite acceptable profits are produced.

The second category of product to be considered for discontinuation are those that are part of an overfilled product line, where sales of one item can come only at the expense of cannibalising sales of others. Further to this unfavourable effect on sales, there is the problem that inventory and distribution costs increase greatly as the product line is extended. It is this dual squeeze on profits in an environment of general rising costs that has led to policies of rationalisation or line reduction.

6. The Branding and Positioning of Products
Kotler uses a definition of *brand* as follows:

'A name, term, sign, symbol or design or a combination of them which is intended to identify the goods or services of one seller or group of sellers, and to differentiate them from those of the competitors'.

He describes a *brand-name* as:

'That part of a brand which can be vocalised'.

Branding is an important part of product planning and involves decisions on which products to brand and how to manage the brands. The use of branding differentiates a product and communicates its attributes in terms of quality, function, physical characteristics and image. The sum of these attributes is often referred to as the *Brand Image*. It is necessary for the company to decide whether to use individual brand names unrelated to the product, for example, Unilever's Walls (ice-cream and meat products), Persil and Radiant (detergents), Stork (Margarine); or whether to use a blanket family brand name such as adopted by Heinz. Alternatively, the company can delegate its branding responsibility by manufacturing for the *own-brands* of retailers and wholesalers.

Having decided its policy on branding, the company must position its brand(s) so as to be distinctive from the competition and attractive to the target market. It is essential that this position is reviewed continuously, and action taken to reposition in response to competitive activity and changing consumer preference.

7. Summary
The product is the most important element of the marketing mix, and product planning decisions are central to the company's development and success. These decisions determine the range of products to be offered, modification of the product line and the image to be adopted.

1. The Advertising Communication Process

Advertising, and indeed marketing, can be viewed as a system of communication between buyers and sellers. The word 'communication' is derived from the Latin *communis*, meaning common. Thus, when an advertiser is communicating, he is establishing 'commonness' with someone, or sharing some knowledge or information.

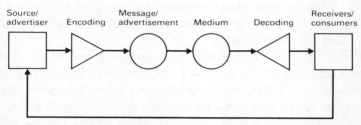

Fig. 11

A model of the advertising communication process is illustrated in Fig. 11.

In advertising, the *source* is an advertiser or advertising agency, who *encodes* the advertising message in words, music or pictures, and places it in an advertising medium. The receivers or target market *decode* the message, by reading, listening, viewing. Feedback consists of sales levels, consumer attitude or awareness, or whatever measurement the advertiser decides to use.

The model indicates the complexity of effective advertising communication. Advertisers must, like teachers, understand their audiences in terms of their interests, language, imagery, attitudes, education and so on. Such information must be applied to the design of advertising messages which must be placed in appropriate media, and there must be accurate feedback, through market research.

Every stage in the model represents a potential barrier to effective advertising communication, and it is all too possible for advertisements to be ignored, misunderstood, forgotten or disbelieved.

Therefore, it is essential that the advertisement meets the following criteria.
(a) Gains the attention of the intended audience.
(b) Is interesting to the intended audience.
(c) Is comprehensible to the intended audience.
(d) Is memorable to the intended audience.
(e) Is credible to the intended audience.

2. Attention and Interest

The first barrier to communication is that the advertisement might not reach the intended audience – there is no point in having the most important message in the world if no one sees or reads it. Gaining attention and interest involves media choice and creative design.

First, unless the media are properly selected, the intended audience will not even have the opportunity to see the advertisement. Thus, for example, an advertisement for detergents is more likely to reach its target – housewives – in the break during Coronation Street than in the racing edition of an evening newspaper.

Second, it is necessary to design an advertisement that is attractive to the audience as, generally, people do not read newspapers or watch television primarily for the advertisements. Moreover, it has been estimated that there can be up to 1,000 advertisements seeking the attention of a consumer on any one day, so those that he or she does see have competed very successfully.

However, in advertising, the single-minded pursuit of attention and interest can lead to the use of irrelevant gimmicks that detract from the overall communication goal by gaining attention for the advertisement rather than for the message; for example, the use of scantily-clad young women in advertisements for almost any product for men. No doubt men look at the advertisements, but it is extremely likely that they notice the woman rather than the message about the product.

3. Comprehension

A barrier to communication occurs if the advertisement is incomprehensible or ambiguous. Anything that is difficult will be passed over, and anything confusing will be similarly ignored or interpreted in any way that makes sense to the audience.

Thus, the simplicity of which advertisements are often accused is invariably necessary in order to make them comprehensible in the crowded and rushed context in which they are seen.

Further, different consumers have different levels of education and understanding and it is essential to speak in the appropriate terminology and language. For example, a motoring enthusiast is likely to understand and appreciate a technical specification, whereas the average motorist would be more interested in simple points of miles per gallon, comfort and style. Again, consumers use different words for the same subject, for example in many households the evening meal is called 'Tea', while in others it is 'Supper' or 'Dinner'.

A major problem in making the message understood as intended arises from the complexities of encoding and decoding. Meaning is conveyed by many factors other than the actual words used. Tone of voice, facial expression and gestures are used to interpret and embellish the message. For example an advertisement for detergent showing a housewife doing her washing will be interpreted differently according to factors such as the housewife's age, clothes and accent, the size and condition of the kitchen and so on.

These 'secondary communication' effects can be so important that they obscure the primary message: the detergent might be rejected because the housewife portrayed was considered 'too posh', 'flashy' or 'scruffy' or because the kitchen looked unitdy, too large or too small. The product is then judged by these characteristics.

4. Memorability
Forgetting the message is another barrier to communication. It is very difficult to make advertisements memorable. Some, such as 'The Man in the Hathaway Shirt', are remembered because of their sheer originality, but the most likely ways to make an advertisement remembered is for it to say something that is important to the audience or is consistent with its current attitudes and, more simply, is frequently repeated.

5. Credibility[1]

Even though an advertisement is seen, understood and remembered in the ways intended, it can fail to communicate at the barrier of being disbelieved. Advertisements that are most likely to be believed are those that agree with the belief structures of the audience. Thus, if people believe that Jaguar cars are expensive to run, advertisements saying otherwise are unlikely to be believed. However, advertisements that say that Jaguars are fast will be believed.

Therefore, to obtain credibility, the advertisement should find and echo some attitude held by the audience, i.e. it must tell people something they want to hear.

6. Conclusion

The advertising communication process is complex, and there are a series of potential barriers to communication. While it is never possible to guarantee that communication will take place as intended, knowledge of the barriers can assist in designing advertisements with the best chance of achieving the communication goal.

Answer 32 **Models of Advertising Effect** Question page 7

---

1. How Advertising Works

There is no generalised answer to the question of how advertising works. The best that can be said is that advertising works in different ways in different situations, and it does not make sense to expect the same pattern for advertising for every product.

Therefore, according to circumstances, advertising can have functions such as:

(a) *To inform*, e.g. about a new product, new features, lower price, etc.

(b) *To turn products into brands*, by creating differentiation between similar products, e.g. detergents.

(c) *To lift products onto a plateau of acceptability*.

1. For a full discussion of credibility in advertising see answer 12.

(d) *To form or change consumers' image of products*, e.g. male toiletries.

(e) *To reinforce existing behaviour*, e.g. an existing brand with a large market share.

There are two distinct approaches to the problem of understanding how advertising works. 'Hierarchical' models state that advertising has to communicate, in order to take the consumer through a series of stages of attitude formation before purchase. 'Sales' models argue that the only function of advertising is to improve sales.

2. The Sales Model

Supporters of this model (usually from outside the advertising industry) argue that the success of advertising can be judged only by the extent to which it increases sales, or at least minimises or reduces sales decline. The problem with this thesis is that the level of sales is affected by such a wide range of factors – other marketing variables, competition and so on – that to relate sales to advertising alone is very likely to be misleading.

Research shows examples of advertising campaigns that have communicated successfully without leading to sales increase, and of products that sold well when the advertising has not communicated, or even when there has been no advertising at all!

Therefore, it is said that sales is a *marketing objective* and advertising's contribution to the achievement of this objective is most validly measured in terms of its success at communication with the target market.

3. Hierarchical Models

Samples of the models that have been developed are shown in Fig. 12. Like all hierarchical models, these have the common assumption that consumers pass through a series of stages to the point of purchase. Despite the apparent differences between these models, all are based on the three stages: *cognitive* (awareness/knowledge), *affective* (liking, preference) and *action/behaviour*.

The models indicate that advertisers should analyse the stage that their target market is at and design advertising accordingly. For example, for a new product, consumers are

	AIDA*	DAGMAR*	Hierarchy of effects	Communications
Cognitive stage	Attention	Awareness	Awareness	Exposure
		Comprehension	Knowledge	Reception
Affective stage	Interest	Conviction	Liking Preference	Attitude
	Desire		Conviction	Intention
Behaviour stage	Action	Action	Purchase	Behaviour

*Acronyms for, respectively: Attention, Interest, Desire, Action; and Defining Advertising Goals for Measuring Advertising Results.

Fig. 12

likely to be at the stage where advertising should concentrate on creating awareness and knowledge of the product. Alternatively a product might be well known but the target market might have a neutral or unfavourable attitude, which advertising should be employed to modify.

4. Usefulness of Hierarchical Models

Whilst these models can assist in the design of campaign plans, they all exhibit certain weaknesses. First, advertising is only one determinant of purchase and favourable attitude towards or conviction about a product depends on a range of factors such as quality, performance, price distribution and competitive products.

Second, consumers do not react as predictably and obligingly as the models suggest. They have their own habits, beliefs and perceptions which they use to interpret advertisements. Thus, there is no guarantee that a consumer will not get 'stuck' at a particular stage or that a buyer who is dissatisfied with a brand can be persuaded to like or repurchase it in the future.

Third, as shown by extensive research over many years, attitude and behaviour are not so correlated that the creation of a favourable attitude necessarily leads to purchase.

Fourth, interest in or conviction about advertising might be caused by having bought the product, rather than the reverse process. For example, recent buyers of new cars tend to be avid and favourable readers of advertisements for the model just purchased.

Fifth, it is unrealistic to expect advertising to make the same contribution to the sale of every type of product. It is plausible that advertising might be a major determinant of the purchase of a toiletry product such as a shampoo but it is most unlikely that even the most convincing advertisement for a car will lead to much more than interest, favourable attitude or further enquiry.

Sixth, for 'low-involvement' purchases where consumers perceive minimum differences between brands, there is none of the lengthy consideration suggested by the models. Instead, consumers go directly from awareness to purchase, without attitude change. In the supermarket, or wherever purchase is made, the consumer recognises the brand, buys it and change in attitude occurs after use. In such cases, the function of advertising is to build up product awareness and to support favourable attitude after purchase.

5. Conclusions

The Sales Model of advertising, whilst attractive in its simplicity and directness, suffers from over-simplification – consumer behaviour and sales depend on a complex process with many factors of which advertising is only one. Neither can Hierarchy of Effects Models provide perfect descriptions of how advertising works because of the range of variables operating in any one purchase and the variations between different types of purchase.

Nonetheless, these models are useful for three reasons.

(a) They provide, within a general framework, an indication of how advertising works and thus emphasise that advertising needs to be systematic and planned.

(b) They identify stages in the advertising process, and thus show that each stage may require a different type of advertising.

(c) They provide an analytical framework for diagnosing the extent to which advertising is achieving its objectives.

Answer 33 **Creating an Advertising Campaign** Question page 7

---

1. Introduction

Rather like medicine, advertising has a range of theorists and practices. As a result, it is misleading to give a definitive answer on how advertising campaigns are created. However, it is reasonably accurate to say that *in most cases* advertising campaigns are developed within a given framework of operation.

The parties involved are: the *advertiser* (and his product or service); (usually) an *advertising agency*; the *media owners*; and the *consumer*. In simple terms, it is normal for the advertiser, termed 'the client', to brief the agency on the advertising required. However, agency/client relationships vary greatly, so that there are enormous differences in the relative initiative and influence exercised; sometimes the advertising agency is indeed an agent, simply carrying out instructions, whereas in other cases the agency determines the campaign, with the client giving approval to the plans put before it.

2. The Campaign Plan

Regardless of the organisational framework, the creation of an advertising campaign involves much more than writing, drawing or filming the advertisements that finally appear. Decisions have to be made in the following areas.

(a) Advertising objectives, or goals

(b) Budget determination.

(c) Media planning.

(d) The advertising message.

(e) The means of assessment.

It should be noted that these are decision *areas* rather than decision *stages*, as in different circumstances the sequence will be altered. In many cases there will be no sequence at all as one stage will overlap with others, and decisions in one area will be retaken following consideration of outcomes elsewhere. Even assessment takes place at a number of stages throughout the campaign.

3. Advertising Objectives

Advertising objectives are central to every element of the advertising campaign. However, there is little agreement on how advertising works, and therefore on the type of advertising objective that is appropriate and valid. For example, some argue that advertising should be judged in terms of its effect on sales, but there are numerous cases where advertising has failed to communicate with the target market, yet sales have increased; and vice versa, probably due to exogenous factors such as price, product quality and competitive activity.

For these reasons, advertising objectives are usually set on the following terms:

(a) *The target*: The people to be reached by the advertising.

(b) *The communication goal*: Such as awareness (of a new product), brand preference (for an existing product).

(c) *Time scale*: For the achievement of the objective.

It is essential that advertising objectives are specific and achievable; for example 'to create within a 12-month period the attitude among at least 50% of ABC_1 housewives that Brand A margarine is a good quality product with strong slimming and health attributes'. Such an objective forms the basis for decision-making in all other areas of the advertising campaign.

4. Budget Determination[1]

Although many textbooks describe methods that companies use to decide how much to spend on advertising, in practice companies seem to evolve methods that are a combination of some or all of these methods. The method that should predominate in the decision process derives from the advertising objective set – the tasks, in terms of the media exposure necessary to communicate the required message to the target market. In the margarine example, where heavy use of expensive media such as television and women's press would be needed, the budget would thus be high.

5. Media Planning[2]

Media planning involves:

(a) *The choice between media*: media selection.

(b) *The timing of the advertisements*: media scheduling.

As indicated in the previous section, the advertising objective forms the basis for the media plan. Media are selected according to:

1. For a full discussion and application of determining the advertising budget see Answer 35

2. For a full discussion and application of media planning, see Answer 37

(a) Their relative cost for delivering the message to the target market.

(b) Their relative capability at communicating the message to the target market.

Costs, invariably compared on a 'cost-per-thousand' basis, are derived from the prices charged by the media-owners and from the readership and viewership figures produced by organisations such as BARB and JICNARS[3]. However these data have shortcomings; for example, in comparing the communication capability of a 30-second television commercial with that of a full page in *Woman's Own*. Such *qualitative* differences are difficult to judge, but must be incorporated into the media selection decision.

The *media schedule* concerns the timing of advertisements in both the short and long term; for example, the time of day, day of the week, season, time of year or the concentration of advertisements in 'burst' or 'continuous' patterns.

6. The Advertising Message

As will be apparent, while the message is necessarily the most visible element of the campaign, it is only one of a number of important elements. As with budget determination and media planning, the advertising message design derives from the advertising objective.

Message design falls into two stages. *Creative strategy* – the concept or theme to be used; and the *creative tactics* – the way(s) in which this strategy will be 'executed' in the finished advertisements. In the margarine example, the *strategy* might be to establish the product's quality/health image by differentiating it as being made only from selected, fibre-related ingredients. The tactics might be to use an appropriate presenter, or a 'slice-of-life' story of two housewives in discussion.

7. Assessment

Advertising assessment (or measurement or testing, as it is also called) should be carried out at all stages of the advertising campaign.

Exploratory research and pretesting assists in the devel-

3. For description of BARB and JICNARS see answer 26

opment of the creative strategy and tactics. *Post-testing* examines the effectiveness of the various advertisements and of the entire campaign *after* appearance.

Again, advertising objectives are central, as it is the success with which the objectives have been achieved that is measured.

8. Summary
Planning and implementing an advertising campaign involves a number of closely related activities and decisions concerning the target market, the amount of money to spend, the advertising message, where and when to display this message and the assessment of the overall effect.

Despite this wide and complex range of action required, the setting of clear objectives makes it possible to approach the decision areas in a way that makes advertising if not scientific, at least systematic.

Answer 34 **Promotional Mix** Question page 8

---

1. Definition and Elements of the Promotional Mix
The promotional mix (sometimes called the marketing communications mix) is the combination of media advertising, sales promotion, public relations and personal selling.

Most companies not only use all of these promotional elements but use them in a particular combination or mix.

Individually, the promotional elements can be defined as follows.

(a) *Advertising*: non-personal persuasive communication in mass media, with the objective of influencing attitudes and behaviour, the design and appearance of which is paid for by the sponsor.

(b) *Sales promotion*: persuasive activities, designed and paid for by the sponsor with the objective of increasing sales directly, rather than as a result of influencing attitude.

(c) *Public relations*: communication, initiated or encouraged, although not paid for or controlled by the sponsor, usually appearing in the editorial columns of newspapers and magazines, and on television and radio, with the objective of influencing attitude and behaviour.

(d) *Personal selling*: personal, persuasive communication, controlled and paid for by the sponsor, with the objectives of influencing attitudes and behaviour and directly increasing sales.

2. Characteristics of each Promotional Mix Element
Each element has a different communication capacity.

Advertising

Because of its many forms, uses and media, it is impossible to generalise about the operation of advertising. (Compare for example, television advertising for a hairspray with technical press advertising for a machine tool.) However, it can be said that advertising can communicate with a very large audience at relatively low cost per head and is the most effective promotional element for creating awareness and brand image. Television is the most effective advertising medium where fairly simple messages are required but, like other national media, is very costly in total terms.

Sales Promotion

Sales promotion campaigns have a much lower cost than advertising campaigns, and can be very effective at prompting product trial and at increasing sales in the short term. Demonstrations and exhibitions can be very useful in increasing awareness and comprehension. However, sales promotion generally does not improve brand image, and sales increases often do not last any longer than the promotion.

Public relations

This has a very low cost and can be more credible (and therefore more effective) than advertising as it represents the opinions of journalists, not advertisers. Because of this control by journalists, the opportunities for its use are limited to occasions that are considered newsworthy by the media. Sponsorship of sporting and cultural events can create awareness and favourable attitude.

Personal selling

Although this is expensive per contact and therefore practicable only for communication with small audiences, because of the personal factor it can be very effective, especially for explaining complex messages.

3. Determining the Promotional Mix

It can be seen therefore that, according to circumstances, the four elements of the promotional mix have different effectiveness at achieving communication and marketing goals. These different circumstances can be analysed by the following factors.

(a) Product Life Cyle.
(b) Product type.
(c) Market size and location.
(d) Competition.
(e) Budget.

4. Product Life Cycle

The Product Life Cycle is a difficult and dangerous subject on which to generalise, and decisions on promotional mix depend greatly on the type of product and type of innovation under consideration[1]. However, in the Introductory and Growth stages when it is necessary to obtain distribution, awareness, trial and repurchase, all four elements of the mix are likely to be required at high levels. At Maturity all elements continue to be used, probably at lower expenditure levels (especially on personal selling). There are changes in design such as the advertising becoming more competition-oriented and sales promotion moving towards attracting buyers from other brands rather than from the ranks of the non-users.

In the Decline stage, all elements of the mix are drastically reduced or discontinued.

5. Type of Product

Product type is a major determinant of the purchase decision process, and the promotional mix should be designed to influence this process in the most effective way.

At one extreme, complex products from machine tools to insurance require a high level of personal selling, backed by sales aids such as catalogues and presentation kits. In these cases, the personal selling can take place at the buyer's home or place of work, but for complex consumer products, especially consumer durables, it is necessary for the personal selling to be done at a retail outlet. Advertising is also nec-

1. For a full discussion of Product Life Cycle, see answer 27.

essary for consumer durables, to establish the brand among the repertoire that is acceptable to buyers. Public relations can be useful for products that are new or have some special feature.

For fast-moving consumer goods however, personal selling is required only for intermediaries, and advertising and sales promotion are of prime importance in influencing the purchase decision. Sales of some products might respond to a high level of service and advice from salesmen before purchase and the availability of extended guarantees after purchase. This has become particularly widespread for consumer durables.

6. Market Size and Location
Large markets such as fast-moving consumer goods can be effectively reached only by advertising and sales promotion. However, public relations might be applicable and some personal selling is necessary to reach the intermediaries, wholesalers and retailers.

Markets with a small number of buyers can be reached by any appropriate specialist media or by direct mail (if suitable mailing lists are available). If sales per customer are high, salesmen can be effective, especially if buyers are not too geographically widespread.

7. Competitors
Often, companies use promotional mixes similar to those of their competitors not for lack of originality but because it is the most logical method. However, a different mix can be more effective, not just because of the novelty but also because of differences in company size, resources and marketing strategy.

8. Budget
A company should either use the correct promotion or save what money it has by withdrawing from markets it cannot afford to be in. However, the words 'correct' and 'afford' are rather subjective in marketing communications. For example, a UK cat food company, dwarfed by the market leaders, decided to pull out of television advertising, although an obvious

medium for this product. As the product was premium quality, the company decided to advertise in women's press, backed by instore merchandising and high-quality promotions, such as offering at reduced price books on cats and cat care.

9 Conclusion

Almost all promotion mixes require the presence of all the promotional elements, although the optimum mix of these elements will vary according to a range of factors. The concept of the 'optimum mix' is in any case somewhat illusory, as its derivation depends on knowledge of the effect on sales of the promotional elements both separately and together.

Unfortunately, as so often with marketing problems, sufficient and adequate information for such measurements is not available. Nonetheless whilst the data available are not perfect, they can contribute to improving decisions about the promotional mix.

Answer 35   **Determining the Advertising Budget**   Question page 8

---

1. Problems in Setting Advertising Budgets

The objective of setting the advertising budget is to reach the optimum relationship between expenditure and sales. The decision is extremely complex for a number of reasons.

(a) The effects of other advertising variables, for example quality of the creativity, the skill of the media buying.

(b) The effects of non-advertising variables: price, product design/quality, packaging, distribution, competitive activity, economic conditions.

(c) The interactive effects of these variables, for example an increase in advertising expenditure might lead to competitive reaction.

(d) The different effects of advertising on different products and markets: compare. for example, detergents and machine tools.

(e) The lagged response of sales to advertising; advertising this year, especially for infrequently purchased products, might not influence sales until next year.

2. Methods for Setting Advertising Budgets

Most marketing and advertising texts examine all or most of the following methods.

(a) Historical
(b) Affordable
(c) Percentage of sales
(d) Competitive parity
(e) Management science
(f) Objective and task.

3. Historical Method

This is a specialised application of a generalised approach to forecasting and planning, and derives from the belief that although the future is difficult to predict. it is fairly easy to know the past. Further, if what happened in the past was acceptable, why not seek to continue this past experience by continuing past behaviour into the future?

Provided that the status quo holds, the method is likely to be successful. However, should conditions change, for example new competitors enter the market or the economy in general declines (or revives), past behaviour is less likely to be appropriate. To some extent this problem can be alleviated by modifying action in the light of changed conditions. For example, last year's advertising budget could be increased for next year by a proportion considered necessary to respond to changed factors such as increased media rates or a competitive product launch.

Nonetheless, the method does not examine whether past decisions were optimal and whilst there is a strong case for maintaining (with appropriate modification) policies that have been successful, the question of whether *other* policies would have been more successful remains unanswered and, indeed, unasked.

4. Affordable Method

This method bases the advertising budget not on the past but on what the company considers that it can afford in the period under review. Thus, if the company is doing well (or expecting to do well) it spends more than if it is doing badly. The main criticism of the method is that it inverts the relationship between advertising and company success, so that the size of the advertising budget is dependent on company performance.

5. Percentage of Sales Method

This method determines the advertising budget as a proportion of anticipated sales and is claimed to have the following advantage. It is a systematic and quantified approach to what many consider to be a particularly unsystematic and unquantifiable part of business. Further, like the affordable method it varies the advertising spending according to revenue and thus is often seen by accountants as a method of controlling the otherwise wayward advertising and marketing departments.

Regardless of the merits of these points, there is little to justify the method. First, it is a further example of irrelevant causality in viewing sales as the cause of advertising rather than vice versa, and consequently, like the Affordable Method, leads to a budget set by the availability of funds rather than the availability of opportunities.

Second, dependence of the budget on annual fluctuations in sales militates against long-range advertising planning. For example, in the early stage of a product's life it is probably necessary to spend a high proportion of sales revenue on advertising in order to establish the product, whereas in the Decline stage a 'harvesting' strategy might require no advertising at all. Third, despite its apparent systematic basis, the Percentage of Sales Method still begs the question by not indicating the appropriate percentage of sales on which the advertising budget should be calculated.

6. Competitive Parity Method

This method determines the advertising budget by matching the advertising budgets of competitors, and is based on the rationale of using collective wisdom and avoiding advertising wars.

Neither of these points is valid. There is no certainty that competitors are more expert about optimum expenditure levels; indeed, they might well be copying you, as the process has to begin somewhere! There is the problem of defining 'the competition', as other companies might differ greatly in size and marketing mix strategies, for example using a low advertising budget but also a low price.

Further, except in industries so collusive as to risk prosecution, it is impossible to obtain accurate figures for advertising expenditure, especially in advance. Lastly, history shows that in practice the Competitive Parity method often leads to advertising wars, as companies seek to protect their positions.

7. Management Science Methods

These methods generally use statistical techniques to measure the correlation between advertising expenditure levels and sales, market share or communication. The major criticism of these methods is that, while it is highly desirable to use a scientific approach to determining the advertising budget, the problem remains of how to obtain appropriate data for the models. The sales effect of advertising varies according to type of product, product quality, market share, competitive activity and so on. Although experiments have been carried out to provide data, it does seem that the range required is so wide that the costs and time involved in the collection make the models unusable.

8. Objective-and-task Method

This method determines the advertising budget by the following process. First, define advertising objectives; second, specify the advertising tasks (the media plan) necessary to achieve this objective. The cost of this media plan equals the advertising budget required.

Whilst there remain problems, such as determining the advertising objective and designing the media plan necessary to achieve this objective, the method is the most useful available. It is systematic and market-oriented in focussing on the use of advertising in the manner most likely to assist in the achievement of the company's marketing objectives. Moreover, the objective-and-task method combines the validity of the management scientists' approach with practicality.

9. Conclusions and Recommendation

In practice, the most practical method of determining the advertising budget, and that adopted by most companies, is a combination of *all the methods*. Thus, a budget is proposed using the objective-and-task method and modified according to experience, what anticipated sales will make affordable and past and expected competitive activity.

---

1. The Advertising Agency in the Advertising System

Advertising agencies are one of the four participants in the advertising system – the others being advertisers, media owners and, of course, consumers. The system and the participants is shown in Fig. 13.

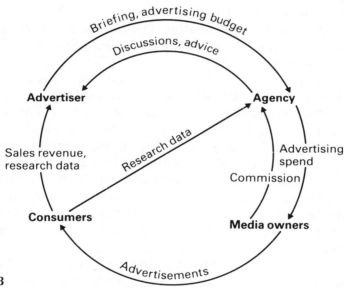

Fig. 13

Originally, agencies' closest relations were with the media owners for whom they acted as agents or brokers selling space to advertisers, and this is the historical basis for their method of deriving the major source of their income from media commission. Legally, the agency is a 'principal' when it buys space (or time) and it is the agency, not the advertiser, that is responsible for the bill.

For the advertiser or client an agency represents a reservoir of skills which even the largest company would find impossible to duplicate at an economic cost. Further, the media commission or discount on the purchase of advertising time and space is usually restricted to established and recognized advertising agencies, which enables agencies to offer their services to advertisers effectively free of charge.

For the media owners, agencies offer economies by bulking together orders and through their familiarity with media-buying methods.

2. Functions of an Advertising Agency

Within the advertising system, an agency has a number of specific and related functions:

(a) *Creating advertisements*: Transforming a marketing objective into words and pictures that successfully communicate with the target market.

(b) *Designing and implementing media plans*: Selecting the advertising media and deciding the size and timing of the advertisements.

(c) *Designing/advising*: On sales promotion, pack design, point-of-sale display, posters and catalogues.

(d) *Advising on marketing and advertising plans*: The degree of involvement depends on the particular agency/client relationship and ranges from the agency simply carrying out instructions to deciding the entire campaign with the client giving approval to plans presented. Only very large agencies are able to operate in this latter way. In such cases the agency would determine the target market, the client's market and product position (and those of competitors) and propose a complete marketing plan, covering not only advertising but also distribution., pricing, packaging and even product redesign. Although such comprehensive advice is now rare, as most advertisers have their own marketing departments and market research data, there is still frequent use of some of these services.

3. Advantages to Clients of Working with an Agency

Regardless of the detailed way that a client and agency work together there are two key features contributing to the relationship.

(a) Agencies are outside the advertiser's firm. The independent perspective they can provide is necessary for the firm wanting a realistic judgement of its advertising and marketing. This independence allows a degree of honest appraisal.

(b) Agencies work for many clients, enabling them to feed into the policies of each a wide range of experience.

4. Organisation of Advertising Agencies

Because of the advantages offered by the advertising agency system, it is a fundamental part in all countries where advertising is at all developed. The exact function and organisation of agencies differs somewhat between countries and even within countries, and it must be emphasised that there are a number of models, often related to the personalities of the founders. Agencies' sizes vary from little more than man-and-a-dog operations to huge international corporations such as J. Walter Thompson and Saatchi and Saatchi.

In recent years there has been a small but significant development of limited service agencies, specialising in media or creativity. Such agencies are used by some of the few advertisers who place their advertising direct rather than through a standard agency, and by full service agencies who subcontract specialist activity to gain specialist expertise or to ease a temporary overload.

Nonetheless most advertising, in the United Kingdom at least, is still placed through full service agencies. A typical organisational structure is shown in Fig. 14.

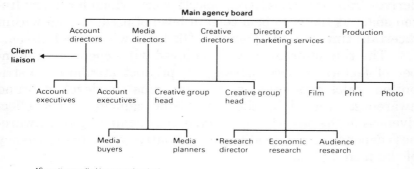

*Sometimes called 'account planning'

Fig. 14

It must be stressed that even in large agencies there are variations to this structure. For example, contact with a large client might be through a Main Board Director. In some agencies the Creative Department is in direct contact with clients, whereas in other cases clients are well insulated from such people. The word 'Director' has specific meanings in advertising agencies. Only at Main Board level does 'Director' have the meaning in terms of status and role that it does in most companies. As can be seen from Fig. 14 there might be a number of 'Creative Directors' or 'Account Directors', each responsible for *directing* that particular aspect of a group of accounts.

5. Summary

Advertising agencies are a crucial element of the advertising system and offer such advantages that they are used for nearly all advertising.

Despite the recent development of specialist, limited service agencies, the majority are still 'full service', offering clients a range of activities from the creation of advertisements to marketing planning.

Answer 37	Media Planning	Question page 8

1. Introduction – defining a Media Plan

A media plan represents the sum of decisions about the media in which to advertise and the size and timing of the advertisements to be used. It is a statement about where and when the advertisements of a campaign will appear. The media plan derives from the advertising objective set, which for a new frozen snack is likely to be a certain level of product trial within a certain time period among $C_{12}DE$ housewives aged 25–54.

The rate of product trial achieved will depend on a number of factors – price, packaging, product attributes, distribution, sales promotion and so on, plus the level of brand awareness created by the advertising campaign. The effectiveness of the advertising campaign at achieving this awareness depends on the quality of the creativity and the efficiency of the media plan.

2. The Media Available

The *classes* of media available are: television, press, cinema, radio, outdoor (transport, posters and aerial). Within each class there are *media vehicles* – particular television regions, individual newspapers and magazines and so on. The fundamental problem of media selection is that each class and each media vehicle has a different capability for communicating an advertising message.

The basis for making such comparisons is an examination of *quantitative factors* and *qualitative factors*.

3. Quantitative Factors

These consist of:

(a) the media habits of the target audience

(b) the comparative cost of these media.

The media habits of the target audience

Which newspapers and magazines do the frozen-snack buyers read? Which television programmes do they watch? Which radio programmes do they listen to? This information on readership and audience size indicates the media most capable of reaching the frozen-snack buyers and is produced by organisations such as JICNARS and BARB.[1] The data show total numbers of individuals and households reached by media, and these totals are broken down by segmentation variables ranging from sex, age, socio-economic group and geographical region to the ownership of various consumer durables.

The figures are expressed in numbers of viewers, listeners and readers and, in the case of television, also as Television Rating points, or TVRs, *one* TVR being 1% of the particular target audience. While the readership and audience figures produced by JICNARS, BARB and the other organisations are continually criticised and challenged within the advertising industry for their alleged inaccuracy, they are very widely used as the basis for media planning.

The comparative costs of media

This is based on the charges made by the media owners and audience sizes and invariably expressed in terms of cost-per-thousand (commonly c.p.t.) (readers, viewers, listeners). The calculation is made using the simple formula:

$$\text{c.p.t.} = \frac{\text{cost of advertisement} \times 1,000}{\text{audience size or readership}}$$

Whilst audience size and readership figures show the absolute numbers of the target market reached, c.p.t. shows the costs of

1. For a full discussion of JICNARS and BARB, see Answer 26.

doing so. For example, a daily newspaper might reach 2.5 million of the target market at a cost for a full-page advertisement of £25,000. A national womens' magazine might reach 1.5 million of the target market at a cost for a full page of £10,000.

The cost-per-thousand figures are:

Daily newspaper $\dfrac{£25,000 \times 1000}{2,500,000} = £10$

Womens' magazine $\dfrac{£10,000 \times 1000}{1,500,000} = £6.67$

4. Qualitative Factors

The comparisons possible with c.p.t. ignore the enormous qualitative differences that make the various media more or less capable of communicating any given message. For example, would a member of the target market for the frozen snack receive the same communication effect from a full-page colour advertisement in womens' specialist press as from a full page in black and white in a larger-format daily newspaper? And how can the effect of either be compared with a 30-second television commercial?

The major quantitative factors that account for such differing effects between media are: creative scope; expertise, prestige and mood; trade reaction; and couponing.

Creative scope

This is determined by the medium's facility for vision, colour, sound, movement and print. All but the last-named are available with television and contribute towards making this such an effective medium by allowing the creation of an infinite range of effects. Using television, it would be possible to demonstrate preparation of the frozen snack, the situation in which it is consumed and the satisfaction of those consuming it.

Expertise, prestige and mood

Advertisements in specialist magazines gain in authority and are likely to be read in a mood created by the publication. Thus, advertisements for the frozen snack might derive authority and be read in a mood of family care if placed in women's housekeeping magazines.

Trade reaction

It is often felt that advertisements directed at consumers can also have an effect on the trade and that the extent of this effect is greater in some media (often television) than in others.

Couponing

Obviously, coupons can be included only in printed media. For a new product such as the frozen snack, coupons or some other inducement to trial might be an important part of the advertising.

Thus, c.p.t. must be weighted by the relevant qualitative criteria when comparing media. While such weights are bound to be determined subjectively and can never be completely accurate, the process is valuable by focussing attention on very important differences between media.

5. The Media Plan

Having compared media for their cost and capability at communicating the required message about the frozen snack to the target market, the final stage of designing the media plan can be undertaken.

This is the decision between the conflicting objectives of:

(a) *Dominance*, by using relatively few, large advertisements in restricted media.

(b) *Increased coverage*, i.e. reaching a greater proportion of the target market by using more media.

(c) *Increased frequency* by using more, smaller, advertisements.

Media planning is bound to be a compromise: to meet any one objective adequately is to fall short on another. The final plan is likely to represent a trade-off between factors such as the length of the campaign, advertisement size, colour/black and white, the use of additional media to achieve extra coverage more frequently, longer bursts and so on.

Those decisions can be taken only in the light of the original campaign and media objectives – the level of brand awareness considered necessary in order to achieve the rate of product trial required.

The decisive factor is the frequency required, i.e. the number of times it is considered that members of the target market should see the advertisement for communication to occur. Although there is no rule on a precise figure that is ideal, many media planners suggest between three and five, depending on the type of advertising message and product. Finding the equilibrium (or rather getting as near as possible) is the result of experience and pretesting the advertising message.

Answer 38   **Sales Promotion**   Question page 8

---

1. Introduction and Definition

Sales promotion covers all forms of non-advertising impersonal promotion paid for by the company. It consists of persuasive activities designed and paid for by the sponsoring company with the objective of increasing sales directly, rather than as a result of influencing attitude.

Sales promotion's distinction from advertising is emphasised by its traditional name of 'below-the-line' drawn by advertising agencies on their invoices to separate sales promotion from the advertising on which they are able to charge media commission. Although sales promotion is distinct from advertising, it often uses advertising to publicise promotional campaigns.

The purpose of sales promotion is to increase sales in the short term as consumers, industrial buyers and retailers respond to inducements such as price reductions, increased quantity for the same price, or the opportunity to obtain free, by competition or at reduced price, another product or service.

Although sales increases caused by sales promotion usually last only as long as the promotion, this is not always the case. Sales promotion can be used to establish new products or to increase the long-term market penetration of existing products.

As there are so many types of sales promotion, it is impossible to generalise about its methods and scope, except to note that:
(a) Its overall objective is usually to complement personal selling and media advertising.
(b) Its effect is to create immediate or short-term sales increase, whereas advertising is usually directed at the long-term goal of influencing buyers' attitudes.

2. Forms of Sales Promotion

Promotions are most frequently used for fast-moving *con-*

142

sumer goods, but many of the techniques are equally applicable to consumer durables, services and industrial goods.

3. Consumer Sales Promotions

On-pack single purchase

Offers related to one purchase, such as a reduction – '5p off'; increased quantity for usual price – '20% extra free'; a 'banded pack' – two for the price of one; or a complementary product, such as a toothbrush given free with a tube of toothpaste; a gift – a sachet of shampoo with a magazine or, one of the earliest forms of sales promotion, a free plastic daffodil with a pack of soap powder.

The objective with such promotion is to obtain an immediate sales increase or trial for a new or existing product, which will lead to adoption.

However, whilst such promotions often produce quite dramatic increases in sales, they tend not to lead to new long-term buyers in mature markets. They attract mainly deal-prone consumers who switch between brands as deals become available. Loyal buyers tend not to change their buying patterns as a result of competitive promotion.

On-pack multiple purchase

Offers related to a number of purchases, of either a single brand or a family of brands such as: 'send 6 packet tops to receive £1' or 'send 6 packet tops and £8.75 to receive this luxury set of cutlery'; or 'send 6 packet tops and answer 3 questions to win a holiday'.

Again, such promotions have the objective of increasing short-term sales, but also are more likely to cause a change in longer-term buying habits; if a consumer has to, and is prepared to, buy a product on six or so occasions, there is a probability of more permanent change to the product. What might also happen, of course, is that consumers who are already loyal buyers will take up the offers, with the effect of receiving a price-reduction on products that they would have purchased in any case.

Money-off on-pack purchase

For the present or next purchase.

Coupons

In newspapers or letter-box delivered. This is a successful method for literally buying short-term sales which tend to last only for the offer, after which buyers revert to previous behaviour. However, the main reason for the decline in popularity of couponing is 'mal-redemption', by which retailers accept the coupons against the purchase of other brands.

Competitions
A method of endless variations from bingo to the Martini competition that offered a Lamborghini – as second prize!

Exhibitions and demonstrations
From the Ideal Home and Motor Show to test-driving cars, in-store demonstrations of how to use a gadget or prepare a food.

Free samples
Small packs of the product letter-box delivered, made available by post or in store, such as food and wine tastings in supermarkets and off-licences.

4. Retailer/Trade Forms of Sales Promotion

Point-of-sale material
Publicity and display material to encourage consumers at the point of purchase.

Merchandising support
Manufacturers' staff visiting stores to assist in display and selling.

Exhibitions and demonstrations
'Trade shows', similar to Ideal Home and Motor Show, but exclusively for retailers and the trade; demonstrations of new products to meetings of retailers.

Discounts and commission
Analogous to the 'money-off' deals in consumer promotions: increased discounts on all purchases or on a scale related to level of purchase.

Competitions
Again analogous to consumer promotions: retailers or their employees qualify to enter and obtain prizes according to sales levels.

5. Industrial Sales Promotion

Exhibitions, Trade Fairs and demonstrations
Discounts and finance
Special prices and loans at favourable rates.

Premiums and inducements
Desk-top or executive gifts, diaries, briefcases, calendars.
Systems and installation support
Free provision of services required to use a product or service.

6. Sales Promotion and the Overall Promotional Campaign

Although media advertising can influence consumers' awareness and attitude, consumer inertia often prevents trial or adoption and therefore some additional incentive such as money-off or free sampling is required.

In established and highly competitive markets, such as shampoo and detergents, where product differentiation is difficult, promotions are used to seek both short-term and long-term sales. While it is often the case that sales levels revert to previous levels after the promotion, the longer-term promotions, such as those requiring consumers to make a number of purchases over time, *can* influence brand loyalty. This is so where loyalty was weak before or where the product being promoted has some objective advantage that is apparent to users only over a period.

Even the short-lived sales increases are often attractive if the company has large stocks or is anxious to regain or maintain market share in the short term. If, as in many markets, all companies are using sales promotion regularly, any that do not will lose market share. Although such market share is 'bought', the price is often comparatively low, as the cost of a national sales promotion is a fraction of that of a national advertising campaign. In addition, a consumer sales promotion affects not only consumers but also the trade whose interest in the brand is increased.

It is essential to note that, despite the undoubted ability of sales promotion to increase sales at short notice and at comparatively low cost, it is not a substitute for media advertising. A product's or brand's long-term future depends on the attitudes and behaviour of the purchasers and cutting back on media advertising to build up short-term sales can lead to a deterioration in consumers' overall impression of the product. A product with a strong brand image can end up being seen as a product that is 'always on offer' and therefore suspect.

Although sales promotion can create immediate sales, only media advertising can create brand image.

---

1. Introduction

In 1983 over £3 billions was spent on advertising in the United Kingdom, representing about 1.3% of Gross National Product. Moreover, advertising is by necessity conspicuous and accessible, so it is not surprising that it is the subject of extreme and polarised opinions, often closely related to political and social values.

Its critics charge it with causing materialism, sexism, cultural pollution and general moral decline, as well as having the economic effects of increasing prices and reducing innovation and competition. Its supporters claim that these undesirable factors existed in society before the appearance of advertising, especially in its modern form, and that advertising is at worst a reflection of society, not an influence. They deny that advertising is harmful economically and contend that it encourages competition, innovation and expanding National Product.

2. Advertising and Price

It is claimed that the very high expenditures on advertising lead inevitably to increased prices as the advertising cost is passed on to consumers. Further, by creating product differentiation and brand loyalty, advertising is said to distort the market and give companies discretion in price-setting. Galbraith has gone as far as to say that advertising is used by companies to 'manage' demand and prices, just as though they were merely company variables. In economic terms advertising moves the demand curve to the right and nearer to a vertical slope, so that price-elasticity is reduced. As evidence the 1973 Monopolies Commission Report on the breakfast cereal market is cited: advertising and promotion 'help to create and maintain the kind of market in which it is possible . . . to have substantial freedom to determine prices'.

In response, supporters of advertising make various counter-claims. First, that the major proportion of advertising expenditure goes towards subsidising the cost of the newspapers, magazines and transport where it appears. In the case of commercial television, radio and 'free-sheet' newspapers, advertising provides these media at no charge. Second, it is said that advertising reduces prices by establishing and stabilising demand so that large and continuous production runs are possible, leading to economies of sale.

Third, it is argued that advertising has a further reducing effect on prices by allowing retailers to lower their margins on advertised products. This is partly because advertised products will have faster turnover rates (than non-advertised products) and partly because they require less selling effort by retailers as consumers are informed about product features by the more efficient means of advertising. The evidence for all this is said to be to compare prices in supermarkets with those in small grocery stores. It is said that even if advertising did raise prices this should not be considered in isolation, but compared with the benefits such as reassurance, confidence and 'psychic' possession utility that comes from purchasing advertised brands.

Lastly, it is asked, if Galbraith is right, and companies can control demand, would there be such a high rate of new product failure and would the sales of once-established products, such as Brylcreem, be allowed to decline?

A response from advertising's critics is that as advertising costs are included in the price of brands, consumers have no choice about paying them. A consumer might not use public transport, watch commercial television or listen to commercial radio, yet he or she still pays the advertising costs when buying advertised products. Moreover, it is pointed out that 'psychic' possession utility is a rather vague concept that is impossible to quantify.

3. Barriers to Market Entry
It is generally agreed that any barriers that inhibit companies from entering markets operate against consumers' interests by reducing both competitiveness and the rate of product improvement and innovation. Critics of advertising claim that the very high levels of advertising expenditure in many mar-

kets act as such a barrier by requiring any prospective entrant to invest not only in the physical development of a product but also in very high advertising and promotional costs in order to establish the product in the market. Referring to the detergents market in 1966, for example, the Monopolies Commission reported that the effect of advertising was to 'create a situation in which even the less successful can earn extremely high profits'.

Supporters of advertising take a contrary view, saying that advertising increases competition and encourages innovation. Advertising is said to allow a company to make a new product known to the widest possible market in a very short time, therefore accelerating payback on the investment. Thus advertising contributes to innovation and the increase of total output and consumer welfare – the process described by Winston Churchill as 'oiling the wheels of industry'.

Critics say that this argument is invalid and that it is possible to find many large markets where, as in the detergents case, there are very high levels of advertising and quite low levels of market entry and innovation. Further, there is very heavy advertising in many markets, such as detergents, chocolate and cigarettes, where total sales are static or even declining. In such cases, no amount of advertising will increase the market size and the aim of the advertising expenditures of individual companies is to maintain present market share or to increase market share at the expense of competitors.

However, the relationship between advertising and innovation, market entry and output remains uncertain. There are undoubtedly cases where advertising is used defensively, for the company's benefit rather than for the consumer, but equally there are cases where advertising is essential in spreading news of an innovation. ('Innovation' meaning in this case a product that is objectively new or improved, rather than a cosmetic relaunch of an existing product.) The Classical Economists attempted to deal with the problem when incorporating advertising into their theory. They distinguished between *informative* advertising, which disseminates information that helps consumers in their buying decisions, and *combative* advertising, by which companies dispute market share. Unfortunately this does not advance the argument very far, as it merely shifts the problem to the stage of deciding in which of the two classifications to place particular advertising campaigns.

4. Conclusion

Two generalisations are possible concerning the effect of advertising on price levels and product innovation. First, any level of expenditure on the most persuasive advertising will not induce consumers to buy a 'bad' product, i.e., a product that consumers do not like, or which has gone out of fashion or which is perceptibly inferior to the competition in some aspect such as quality or price.

The fallacy of Galbraith's claims about demand management can be seen in the very companies he cites – the problems experienced in the 1970s by General Motors, Ford and Chrysler in the face of competition from Japanese and European car companies. No level of advertising could make up for the fundamental marketing problem of the absence of products that were attractive to the market.

Second, it is impossible to generalise further about the effect of advertising on price and innovation. The effect varies from case to case and depends on a range of factors such as Product Life Cycle stage, opportunity for differentiation and social and economic factors. For every case, such as corn flakes or baked beans, where advertising might appear to be supporting a static market (although both of these have seen extensive private-label activity) there are others, such as muesli cereals and instant noodles where advertising has made a major contribution to consumer awareness and market expansion.

Answer 40   **Pricing a New Product**   Question page 9

1. Factors in the Pricing Decision

There are two main sets of circumstances in which most companies have to take pricing decisions. First, when a new product is developed. Second, when there is some change in the environment that affects production or sales. This can result

from a rise in the cost of some element of the production process, or a decrease in demand, caused by factors such as a new
competitor in the market, a change in buying patterns or
economic recession.

Pricing decisions can be distinguished between *pricing
strategy* – the task of defining the price range that would support sales and profit objectives and the positioning of the product in the market; and *pricing tactics*, the task of setting a
specific price.

There are three general factors involved in the pricing
decision.

(a) *The market factor*, of gaining consumer acceptance and
    achieving sales and market share objectives.
(b) *The company factor*, of managing production capabilities
    and costs so as to achieve the difference between cost and
    price that is necessary to meet the profit objective.
(c) *The competition factor*, of achieving sales objectives in the
    face of competitive products and the policies of other
    companies.

2. The Market Factor

This is comprised of the product's distinctiveness (as compared
with the competition), its attractiveness to consumers and the
role of the dealers to be used.

For a product with no distinctiveness – a 'me-too' copy of
a product or products already established in the market –
there is very little choice about price. The product must be
priced at, or preferably below, competitors' prices if it is to
have any chance of selling. The mini television, however, is
completely distinctive, so that buyers have very little with
which to compare it. As a result, the company has a very wide
choice of pricing strategies, ranging from a *skimming* or very
high price, aiming the product at a small price-inelastic market segment, to a *penetration* or very low price aiming the
product at the widest possible market.

The product's attractiveness to buyers is expressed in the
anticipated *adoption curve*. This can vary between a very slow
rate of adoption with a low eventual penetration level (suggesting a skimming price) and rapid and total penetration of
the entire market (suggesting a penetration price).

Estimating the price that buyers would be prepared to pay for a new product and the likely penetration is not easy. Although there are various research techniques that can be used, there are often surprises; for example, companies in the market and independent observers were astonished by the very high adoption rate of video recorders in the United Kingdom in the early 1980s, in a time of severe economic recession.

The last aspect of the market factor is distribution. Price has to be decided not only in terms of what the consumer will pay, but also the margin to be offered to dealers. All other things being equal, this should be at least the same as that offered on competitive products. For a new product, a higher margin might be necessary to compensate retailers for higher selling costs and the risk of slow turnover and, in the case of a product failure, stocks that can be sold only at a reduced price.

3. The Company Factor

This is concerned with output level capabilities, production costs at various output levels and general company policy and image.

The feasible production capacity in the long and short term will determine the sales levels that can be sought. A penetration price strategy that attracts high demand without a matched supply of the product will lead to dissatisfaction at both dealer and consumer levels.

Concerning costs, it is obvious that in the long run at least these must be less than selling price. Moreover, significant variations in costs at various output levels might well influence the pricing strategy adopted. If, for example, production of the mini television is subject to economies of scale, this will encourage management to consider a penetration price. It should be noted that, in this context, 'cost' covers not only production but also marketing and distribution.

The third company factor, company policy and image, will influence pricing strategy in that the price set must be consistent with the general objectives and direction of the company. For example a consumer electronics company like Sony, with a reputation for products towards the top end of the market, would not want to price a new product at a level that had any implications of inferiority or cheapness.

4. The Competitive Factor

The distinctiveness of any product is under continual threat of erosion or destruction from the entry to the market of rival products. This threat might be mitigated by patents (as in the cases for many years of Xerox and Polaroid) or by simple absence of other companies with the necessary technology or other resources (as in the case for many years of Seiko).

In the absence of such security however, companies often seek to protect their innovations through marketing, particularly price. Therefore, to discourage competitive market entry, the mini-television manufacturer might set price very low, hoping to signal to other companies that profits in the market will be hard-come by, because of low margins and aggressive marketing.

5. Marketing Strategy

Having analysed these three sets of factors, the company can progress towards deciding a marketing strategy. (As price is a component of marketing, decisions on marketing strategy are taken first, and the price set must be consistent with the other marketing mix variables and with overall marketing objectives).

The formulation of marketing strategy for the mini television involves decisions on the target market to aim at and the product's position in the market. For example, the television could be sold as a fun product for children and young people, or as a hi-tech executive accessory. Adoption of the former strategy would depend on high production capacity, low unit costs at high output levels and consistency of this policy with company image. (A way round the company image problem is to launch the product under a different brand name, as Seiko did with Pulsar, although this policy can cause further problems, such as diseconomies in advertising and distribution. In practice, however, companies usually develop products that are consistent with corporate objectives.) Referring to cost, it should be emphasised that low production costs at any level do not mean that the company should follow a cost-plus policy and set a low price. Depending on the preferred competitive stance and what the market will pay, low costs could be coupled with high price to give a high profit margin. With such a policy, however, it is necessary to be able to justify the profit margin to possible inquiries from consumer groups or government.

6. Price Set
Within the broad parameters set by the marketing/pricing strategy, the price set will be influenced by factors such as necessary dealer margins (referred to under the market factor), the need to meet a psychological price, for example under £50 or under £100, and any promotional objectives such as special prices for a limited period to attract attention or encourage opinion leaders to purchase.

7. Conclusion
The price set for the new mini television will be determined largely by the marketing strategy adopted. This marketing strategy in turn is determined by analysis of a range of factors both internal and external to the company.

Answer 41   **Price as an Index of Quality**   Question page 9

1. Introduction
Although economists have been writing about price for almost two centuries, more recently it has been noticed that consumers do not always act with total rationality and that psychology is useful in marketing management's task of understanding consumers in their approaches and attitudes to price. A particular application has been to consumers' perception of the relationship between quality and price.

This has the very serious implication that demand curves slope upwards to the right (rather than the conventional downward slope of economic theory), from which it can be concluded that the higher that price is raised, the greater the amount sold. While this is intuitively implausible, commonly used phrases such as 'You don't get anything for nothing', 'You only get what you pay for' and 'Quality costs', certainly indicate that some consumers, at least, see quality as a variable dependent on price. It is to investigate this contradiction that psychological theory has been developed and psychology-based market research undertaken.

2. Reasons for Judging Quality by Price

In an early article, Tibor Scitovsky,[1] an economist, theorised that in many cases consumer expertise had declined because of:

(a) *The wide range of products available*: Consider, for example the choice of foods available in a superstore.

(b) *The complexity of these products*: This applies not only to high-technology products, but also to groceries and toiletries: consider the chemical formulations referred to in the advertising and packaging of products like shampoos and margarine.

(c) *The speed of innovation*: Again not only in high-technology products: consider the developments in wholefoods.

(d) *The policy of advertisers*: While companies might not set out to deceive, each advertising campaign necessarily emphasises the attributes of a single product with the result that consumers receive a series of conflicting messages about products that might well be similar.

Because of the consequent inability to judge quality from the attributes of products, consumers turn to other signs, including price. This approach is not necessarily irrational, as it is quite likely that price is determined by the forces of supply and demand. Better quality products are likely to cost more to buy because they usually cost more to make. Moreover, consumers might justifiably feel that prices operating are the outcome of the collective experience and behaviour of consumers, and that 'everybody can't be wrong!' For example, although many people have never been in a Rolls-Royce let alone owned one, it is generally thought to be 'the best car in the world', not only because it is the most expensive, but also because those who are in a position to know and choose – film stars, Royalty, chairmen of large companies – tend to buy Rolls-Royces.

3. Price and Risk Reduction

Price is most likely to be used as an index of quality when:

(a) Consumers perceive risk in the purchase, and wish to reduce or avoid this risk,

1. Tibor Scitovsky: 'Some Consequences of the Habit of Judging Quality by Price', *The Review of Economic Studies*, 1944–5, Vol. Xll (2), Number 32

(b) There is an absence of other indices by which risk can be reduced or avoided.

4. Consumers' Perception of Risk in the Purchase

In consumer behaviour, risk is defined as the prospect that a purchase will result in loss or some other unwanted consequences. In other words, the consumer perceives a possibility that the purchase will not work out as he intends. The degree of this risk derives from both consumer and product factors. Some consumers are more cautious than others and therefore perceive risk where the more confident or carefree would not.

Similarly, products vary in the risk involved in their purchase according to a range of factors, chiefly:

(a) *Their novelty to the buyer*: consumers know less about new or rarely purchased products than about those which are bought frequently.
(b) *Complexity*: complex products are more difficult to assess and have more to go wrong.
(c) *Cost*: the higher the cost, the greater the risk, as there is more at stake.
(d) *Conspicuousness*: products with high visibility involve the risk of looking foolish to others if the purchase turns out to be a mistake.

5. Absence of Other Indices

Price is only one means of risk reduction and tends to be used when other indices are absent or confusing. These other indices include previous experience with a brand, reputed brand name, reputation of the retail outlet selling the product and product design and appearance. Research studies have shown price being used as an index of quality for products such as fabrics (where, to the average consumer, good quality products are indistinguishable from inferior quality) and mothballs, where again little is known about the product.

Price is also used in less obscure purchases, where other indices are available, but tend to cancel one another out. For example, when confronted with a range of shoes of equivalent-level brands in the same shop, a consumer might decide against buying the cheapest as a form of insurance.

6. The 'Normal' or Acceptable Price

To return to the question of the upward sloping demand curve, whilst consumers might not buy the cheapest product available, neither do they buy the most expensive. In fact, consumers establish a price or 'price band' within which products are considered to be of acceptable quality. This price is based on a combination of the consumer's financial resources, utility for the product and knowledge of similar products. For example, a man might establish the price band within which he considers stereo systems to be of acceptable quality, as £350–£450. To this man, the further a stereo is priced below £350 the more inferior and unacceptable it is likely to be. Conversely, the further a stereo is priced above £450 the better it is likely to be, but not in a way that would justify purchase for him; such systems would be considered 'extravagant' or 'very good, but not worth the extra'. Assuming this consumer to be typical of a sizeable market segment, if not of the entire market (which will be composed of segments, each with its own price band) a notional demand curve can be drawn as

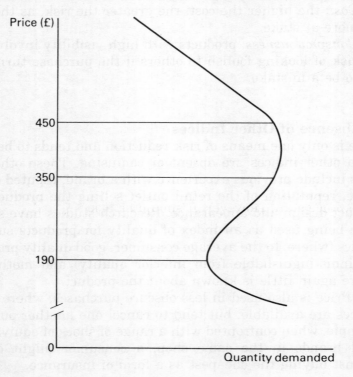

Fig. 15

156

shown in Fig. 15. It will be noted that the number of consumers in this market segment prepared to buy decreases as the price drops below £350, but increases again below £190 at which point they might be prepared to 'take a chance'.

7. Conclusion

It must be emphasised that price is one of a *number of indices* used by consumers to judge quality. In the market place, products of good quality not only have higher prices, but also look better and are sold in better outlets and *are* better than cheaper products. Stories of the sales of products increasing following a price increase should be treated with some scepticism. In fact, when companies seek to increase sales, one of the tactics used is to reduce price rather than increase it.

The psychology of retailers' 'Sales' illustrates the price/quality relationship. When a stereo system is reduced from £400 to £300, the retailer hopes that the quality implication is that this is still a £400 stereo, but now available at £300.

Thus, marketing management needs to note the circumstances in which price is an index of quality, and also the requirement for the price set to be consistent with the overall marketing strategy.

Answer 42   **Channel Development**   Question page 9

---

1. Superstores and Channel Development

The term 'superstore' is used to describe supermarkets with more than 25,000 square feet of selling space. Their development began in the United Kingdom in the North during the 1970s under such names as ASDA and Kwiksave. By the late 1970s, superstores were being opened in the South, not only by ASDA, but also by Sainsbury and Tesco.

In channel development terms, superstores illustrate the drastic change in the balance of power between manufacturers and retailers. Until about 1950, the very large manufacturers with management expertise and big advertising budgets dominated the small and unsophisticated retailers. Well before the appearance of superstores this state had changed, with very large and expert retailers becoming as powerful as, if not more than, the manufacturers.

Superstores indicate the new financial resources, expertise and confidence of retailers.

A result of these changes has been that manufacturers no longer 'manage' 'their' channels of distribution. Manufacturers now have to establish consumer preference for their brands, in order to persuade retailers to allocate shelf space and display.

2. The Channel of Distribution

The development of superstores (and other types of middlemen) is best understood within the general framework of the development of channels of distribution. A channel of distribution can be described in terms of either the *participants* or the *functions*, as shown in Fig. 16.

PARTICIPANTS
Manufacturer – Wholesaler – Retailer – Consumer

FUNCTIONS
Goods and Services ...... Information flow .... Consumption
.... Product flow ....
.... Title flow ....

The channel of distribution

Fig. 16

The range of participants can vary between all, in the case of confectionary sold through CTN's,[1] to virtually none, in direct selling and mail order. The range of functions can be grouped under three 'flows'.

(a) *Information flow*: The flow of information to and from the consumer, carried out by advertising, salesmen, packaging, display and market research.

(b) *Product flow*: The inventory, handling, transport and storage of products and bulk buying.

(c) *Title flow*: The passage of ownership and attendant risk.

Development in many areas of distribution, especially supermarkets and superstores have been characterised by two factors.

1 Confectioners, Tobacconists and Newsagents.

158

(a) *The 'shrinking' of many functions* by increased efficiency and the application of technology.

(b) *The transfer of functions* between participants.

3. The 'Shrinking' of Functions

A major attraction of the superstore derives from the economies of scale that apply to retailing, especially of food. It has been demonstrated that there is a linear decline in wage costs as a percentage of sales associated with increases in store size. Large stores facilitate not only more efficient division of labour, but also economic use of mechanisation and technology for stock handling and control and the packing and labelling of fresh foods. The most recent example of this is EPOS – electronic-point-of-sale – which reduces labour requirements both at the checkouts and also for stock control and reordering.

Improved transport has made it possible to have fewer warehouses and lower stock levels.

4. Transfer of Functions

The development of supermarkets and superstores has involved the disappearance of many separate wholesalers and the acquisition of their functions by retailers. Because of increased financial resources, increased size and decreased number of outlets, retailers have in many cases taken over the remaining wholesaling functions.

Some functions have been transferred out of the traditional distributive chain. Much of the information previously given by retailers now comes from advertising and packaging, and some financing has been taken over by banking and credit cards. A shopper is more likely to spend £50 on a single shopping trip when she has a bank account and knows that cheques are accepted. In addition, some large food outlets, particularly frozen-food shops, accept payment by credit card, which not only dispenses with the need for cash but also allows the shopper to spread the cost of a large purchase over an extended period.

5. Transfer of Functions to the Consumer

Superstores are based partly on economies of scale and the application of technology, and partly on the ability and willingness of consumers to take on additional functions and tasks in return for benefits.

One of these functions is transport. The concept of superstores is that they are very large and few in number. Whereas the old 'corner shop' brought goods to the consumer, superstores require consumers to come to the goods. They rarely draw much of their custom from within walking distance. Indeed, many are deliberately built away from centres of population to obtain the necessary large site at a low property cost.

Users of superstores have to have cars not only for access but also to transport the large quantities of goods that are a feature of less frequent shopping. Moreover, by buying in this way, consumers are assuming some of the finance and risk-taking function by holding considerable stocks. Supermarket/superstore customers take over the function of informing themselves about products, instead of obtaining advice from butchers, greengrocers and so on.

Lastly, they agree to buy in standardised, prepacked quantities.

Although many of these features are to be found in supermarkets, superstores represent a more extreme form, and superstores have developed from the preparedness of many consumers to take on certain distribution functions in exchange for the benefits of lower prices, wider selection and the convenience of one-stop shopping.

6. Extension of the Superstore Concept to Non-food Retailing

To some extent this extension has already occurred. A large number of furniture and carpet sales now go through a few, very large warehouse-type outlets, inevitably sited away from other shops and frequently from public transport. Consumers are expected to transport themselves to the store and to transport their purchases home, which in the case of furniture is usually in flat-packed form, to be assembled by the purchasers. Usually, such outlets have very limited service, with staff employed mainly to organise stock control and the movement of goods purchased from the warehouse to a collection point.

Similar types of outlet have a large share of the electric consumer durable market, and have been introduced to the do-it-yourself area, with large stores offering standardised prepacked products selected by self-service.

The major limiting factor on the growth of superstores is the extent to which consumers feel that they are the appropriate environment for different types of shopping. To date, 'glamourous' products such as clothes and records are sold in large, self-service outlets, albeit usually located in shopping centres. The same is true for complex, costly products, such as cameras and hi-fi, where consumers might be expected to require advice and service.

No doubt some consumers will continue to prefer to shop in small, local shops which offer service, advice and an ambiance not possible with a superstore, even if this results in higher prices.

It is the size and resilience of this market segment that will determine superstore penetration.

Answer 43 Physical Distribution Question page 9
Management

---

1. Physical Distribution Management

Physical distribution management (PDM) is the range of activities concerned with planning and implementing the efficient movement of goods and raw materials – both inwards to the point of manufacture and outwards to the consumer. Thus, PDM requires integration with all parts of the company – production, finance and personnel – as well as marketing. As distribution costs have been estimated at 20% of total costs, it is a very important area, and any savings will contribute significantly to improved business performance.

2. The Elements of Physical Distribution Management

Physical distribution management is connected to all parts of the organisation's operations. For example, the speed with which it can meet customers' orders affects sales and marketing; the size of the inventories kept affects production.

Kotler[1] identifies 'at least fourteen tasks that are in-

1. Kotler, P.: 'Marketing Management', Fourth Edition, Prentice Hall 1980, pages 449–450

volved in physical distribution'. However, the main elements can be described as follows.

Transportation

This involves decisions between modes – air, rail, road, water; and between ownership or leasing of vehicles and the use of outside contractors. One factor in the decision is the product; for perishable products a high-cost mode is justified by speed of delivery; for small volumes, air freight might be economical, and for quite high volumes road might be preferred to rail because of greater reliability. For grocery distribution there appears to be a trend towards contract road carriers, as use of a manufacturer's own fleet can be very expensive in the absence of back-loads.

Warehousing and materials and goods handling

This involves decisions on the number, size, location and design of warehouses, and the systems for sorting, retrieval and recording movement and the use of mechanisation and technology.

Inventory

This involves decisions on the stock levels necessary to meet the customer service objective. The important variables are the customer order quantity, frequency and regularity of orders and delivery times offered. If delivery time is the same as the production cycle, virtually no stock is required and if customers order small quantities regularly, stock levels can be comparatively low. If customers expect to be able to get immediate delivery on any order size at any time, stock levels will have to be high to accommodate sudden surges.

Customer service level

From the customers' viewpoint, service can mean various things – speed of delivery, willingness to meet emergency needs and to exchange goods, availability of repair and service outlets and so on. With 'convenience' products, continuous availability at a wide range of outlets is essential. If there is no stock of a particular brand of confectionery, most consumers will select a competitor rather than search in other shops.

High service levels imply high costs. To give same-day delivery to every part of the country is likely to require special journeys with small loads from a large number of warehouses, each with high stocks.

3. Total Distribution Costs

Decisions about any single element of the distribution system affect not only the entire system but also other functions within the company. Arriving at a total system cost requires decisions to be made on the possible trade-offs between and within distribution activities.

Transport – inventory – materials handling trade-off
Fast transport, e.g. airfreight, costs more than road or rail but reduces costs of inventory and protective packaging.

Warehouse – transport trade-off
Warehouses are subject to considerable economies of scale, so that decreasing the number of warehouses decreases costs. However, this also reduces transport distances and costs and improves delivery times to customers.

Order processing – inventory trade-off
A more sophisticated order processing system might be more expensive (although it might *not*, if computerisation creates large labour cost savings). In any case it can reduce inventory costs by giving more accurate stock control and faster dispatch.

Product line – inventory trade-off
The larger the product line offered, the higher the inventory costs. The importance of this relationship was seen early on by Marks and Spencer, who stock only relatively few, fast-selling products rather than follow the attempt at comprehensiveness that contributed to the problems of Woolworth.

4. Physical Distribution Objective

The company needs to decide between this wide range of trade-offs and to formulate its physical distribution objective. Much data for this decision derives from product factors. For example, in the transport–inventory trade-off, products that are light, valuable, perishable or fragile will be more economic to move by fast though expensive means such as airfreight. Flowers are often sent this way, as is electronic equipment, such as computers, which although heavy is highly breakable and expensive to leave to long-term sea journeys and dock handling.

An objective based on cost factors alone is likely to result in infrequent deliveries from a very few large warehouses. This might be good for costs but is certain to be very bad for sales, and therefore it is necessary to include the concept of level of customer service.

Taking customer service as a single objective will have the opposite effect of the objective of lowest cost. Harrod's celebrated willingness to deliver a single loaf of Hovis to Brighton was excellent for customer service, but devastating for distribution costs. In contrast, Marks and Spencer not only offer a selected product line, but also do so in relatively few, generally large outlets. This contributes to distribution economies which can be passed on in the form of lower prices.

The optimum service level is that which produces the greatest difference between cost and revenue. Clearly this need not be the highest level of service, as the revenue lost by not offering delivery of low-value individual items to Brighton might well be considerably less than the savings in cost. The company's task is to establish the relative importance to the target market of the service factors – delivery, product range, and so on, compared to the service being offered by competitors.

The company then decides on a customer service mix that is competitive and viable. In this it might be possible to persuade customers to accept the mix that best suits the company, and this does not imply intimidation or lack of consumer-orientation. For example, if small orders or orders at short notice are expensive to service because of handling or inventory costs, customers can be encouraged to plan and order more systematically, either by penalties on uneconomic orders, or discounts on orders that are the least costly to process. In fact, this is no more than an application of the credit collection principle of allowing a reduction in invoice value for payment within 30 days.

5. Summary
Physical distribution is an area of high potential cost savings, improved customer satisfaction and competitive effectiveness. The physical distribution concept calls for decisions within each part of the system to be taken within a unified framework. Having achieved this, attention can be given to the primary task of designing a system that minimises the cost of providing a given level of customer service.

1. Introduction

Sales representatives can be among the most productive and
expensive of a company's assets. Whilst the topics of selling
techniques and motivation rightly receive much attention, organisation of the sales force is at least equally important an
aspect of the company's personal selling activity.

The first task for the company is to decide the role and
objective of the sales force. For example, are the goals short-
term, such as generating the highest possible sales from existing customers; or longer-term, such as increasing the number
of accounts or providing service and advice to customers; or
more marketing-related, such as maximising profits?

Having established the objective, the company needs to
decide:
(a) the number of salespeople to employ
(b) the methods and structures by which they are to be
    organised.

2. Sales Force Size

Although at any one time the sales force size is fixed, the opportunity and need to vary this size occurs when staff leave
and sales expand or contract. The two major methods available to the food company (or indeed *any* company) are: *workload* and *sales potential or productivity*.

3. Workload

This is an objective-and-task method which has the principles
of equalising the workload of sales representatives and matching the number of salesmen to the total workload.

The first stage is to segment customers by annual sales.
For the food company this might be as follows:

Segment A: 10 customers – sales per annum over £200,000
Segment B: 40 customers – sales per annum £100,000 –
£199,999
Segment C: 50 customers – sales per annum less than
£100,000

The second stage is to decide the number of calls required annually by each account in each segment. This is multiplied by the number of accounts, as follows:

Segment A: 10 customers × 30 calls = 300
Segment B: 40 customers × 20 calls = 800
Segment C: 50 customers × 8 calls = 400

Therefore the total number of sales calls required a year is

300 + 800 + 400 = 1,500.

Third, the number of salesmen required is calculated by dividing 1500 by the annual call rate per salesman. Assuming that a salesman can make 15 calls a week, for 45 weeks a year, then the number of salesmen required is:

$$\frac{1,5000}{15 \times 45} = 22.2 \text{ or } (22 \text{ in round figures})$$

Clearly, the system is dependent on accurate information about the number of calls required by each customer and the number of calls possible for each salesman. This information is likely to be available within the company, or certainly should be, as it is basic to planning and costing all aspects of sales activity. The system shows the number of salesmen required to maintain the current level of sales, and indicates how the sales effort could be increased by using additional salesmen specifically for new business, or to allow all salesmen to seek new business from new or existing customers.

4. Sales Potential

Whilst the workload method is simple, it is oriented to sales rather than profit. The sales potential method of deciding sales force size provides for influence over profits as well as sales.

The method is based on measuring the sales productivity of salesmen in areas of different potential. It has been found that a salesman can produce higher sales from an area of greater potential, but that these higher sales are not proportionate to this greater potential. For example if Area A represents 2% of the company's potential annual sales, a salesman might produce from it sales of £500,000, if Area B represents 4% of the company's potential annual sales, the same salesman or one of equivalent abilities will not produce £1 million, but more likely, £750,000.

Therefore, if the company employed 50 salesmen, of the same abilities and each with similar sales territory accounting for 2% of the company's sales potential, total annual sales would be:

£500,000 × 50 = £25 million

If 25 equal-ability salesmen were employed, each with a 4% of sales potential territory, total annual sales would be:

£750,000 × 25 = £18.75 million

The larger the sales force used, the more intensive the sales effort and the higher the sales. However, larger numbers of salesmen (and higher sales) might not lead to higher profits, and by estimating sales revenue and costs for various numbers of salesmen the most profitable size of sales force can be determined.

The sales force size decided on might be influenced by company objectives other than short-term profit. For example, if the company wished to increase business, and considered that extra salesmen would assist in the achievement of this objective, a sales force of temporarily uneconomic size might be used as an investment in a future sales increase.

5. Sales Force Organisation
Sales force organisation involves deciding:
(a) sales force structure
(b) sales territory design.

6. Sales Force Structure
The common bases for sales force structures are: geographic, product and *customer*.
Geographic
This is a simple and frequently used method and has a number of advantages. First, it gives salesmen a clear definition of their responsibilities and encourages a high level of effort and commitment for what the salesman identifies as his own territory or 'patch'. Second, salesmen are given the maximum opportunity to become familiar with customers and their re-

quirements. Lastly, and very practical, the costs and time taken by travelling are minimised.

Product

The geographic structure works well unless the company's products are so complex, unrelated or numerous that it is impossible for a salesman to have the necessary level of understanding. Thus, if the food company's range extended from basics such as frozen fish fingers to specialised cooking ingredients such as herbs and spices, it might be decided to set up a separate sales force for each product line. Unfortunately, a sales force structured by product has disadvantages if the separate product lines are bought by the same customers. First, more salesmen are required, as travelling time is increased by the need for different salesmen to cover the same routes. Second, the possibilities for establishing contacts are less than for a single salesman spending more time with each customer. Third, customers can become confused or irritated by having to see different salesmen for what they might regard as similar products from the same firm.

Customer

Separate sales forces can be set up for different industries, markets, customers and new business. The main advantage is to give salesmen the maximum knowledge of customer needs, and the main disadvantage is the likelihood of extended travelling. It is not always possible to find relevant criteria by which to separate markets; the food company might sell only to supermarkets. If it sells to different types of retailer, say supermarkets, chemists, health food shops, CTNs[1] and also to industrial buyers such as caterers, then some separation of the sales force might be appropriate.

7. Sales Territory Design

In deciding the size and shape of its sales areas, the food company should consider these factors.

(a) The need for simplicity and ease of administration and sales estimation.

(b) The need to minimise travelling time.

(c) The need to produce viable sales areas.

Unfortunately, traditional geographic areas such as postal dis-

1. CTN – Confectioner, tobacconist, newsagent.

tricts, towns or counties are unlikely to make suitable sales areas. Thus, areas have to be constructed, and two methods are the previously mentioned 'sales potential' and 'workload'.

The former method has a beneficial effect on salesman monitoring and motivation, as persistent differences in sales levels indicate differences in the efforts and ability (and probably earnings) of salesmen. However, the method is complicated by variations in population density, as areas of varying sales potential have differing travelling requirements.

The workload method deals with this problem. For example, a sparsely populated area, such as the Lake District, might be an area for one salesman although its population and sales potential are half that of a much smaller area such as South Manchester. This method works well, provided that salesmen's pay is not heavily determined by commission.

Clearly, there is no neat solution to a problem with so many variables, and it is necessary to accept and allow for anomalies. Even with areas of equal size and sales potential, salesmen will consider that some are easier, because of traffic densities, or more attractive because of type of customer and environment, and so on.

The answer is to adapt the solution to the problem, rather than vice versa. Some salesmen might prefer certain areas but for areas that are generally agreed to be difficult, additional incentives can be made. The commission for country areas can be different than for town areas. Provided that these differences are known and explained to all, and salesmen have the opportunity of taking areas they prefer, disputes should be minimised, if not eliminated.

8. Conclusion

Although many sales forces develop in Topsyish fashion, it is important to review regularly both the size and structure according to the needs of company products and customers and the supervision and motivation of salesmen.

1. Introduction
The major tasks of managing any sort of staff are to:
(a) attract good people
(b) motivate and develop them
(c) evaluate and improve performance
(d) keep them from leaving.
These factors apply equally to field sales staff as to any other
type of staff, yet it is generally thought that the management
of sales staff is different from the management of any other
type of employee. Certainly, there is the difference that the
activity of field staff cannot be observed directly. It can, however, be monitored continuously by use of a reporting system.
Nevertheless, many companies use a commission system of
payment by sales results as a means of attempting to ensure
a continuous and high level of effort from salesmen. Other
companies have found that the carrot of increased money does
not necessarily lead to increased motivation.

   The range of payment systems extends from salary only
to various combinations of salary and commission to commission only. Each method had advantages and disadvantages.

2. Salary Only
A major advantage of this method is that it provides salesmen
with a regular income. After all, salesmen are just like other
employees in having regular bills to pay – mortgage, rates,
housekeeping and so on. A further advantage is that the
method is simple to operate and minimises the possibilities of
confusion and disputes about the size of the monthly pay che-
que. For sales management, the system gives freedom to direct
and alter sales duties without incurring strong opposition
from the sales force. For example, company policy or a new
product launch might require salesmen to concentrate on customer service or efforts that will not lead to sales until some
considerable time in the future. Similarly, salesmen are not
encouraged towards short-term personal goals, such as high-
pressure selling, which might be contradictory to company
objectives.

However, the method gives no financial incentive, which does not suit the achievement and reward system of many salesmen. In addition, the tasks of supervision and motivation fall entirely on management.

3. Commission Only

Clearly, this method offers the greatest financial incentive and, in theory at least, can be used to direct salesmen's efforts between different activities and products. In practice, however, it is the commission-only method that can lead to the company having least control over the salesforce. The type of salesmen attracted by this sort of payment method are bound to be independent – almost a cowboy type – and likely to resist any attempts to alter their basis of payment. Even if the change is explained as advantageous, such salesmen tend to be very suspicious of any changes in an area so fundamental to their livelihood. Furthermore, as they are so highly motivated by money, they are likely to leave at short notice for any alternative employment that offers a bigger income.

An apparently cynical advantage claimed for this method is that it reduces the company's selling expenses when sales revenue decreases. A final disadvantage is that it is costly to administer and can lead to disputes over the amount of commission due.

4. Salary and Commission Combined

This method does have the advantage of compromise and is the one most used. It gives management some freedom of control whilst retaining some element of financial incentive.

5. Selecting a Payments Method – the Information Available

It would appear that the information available on payments methods for salesmen is so conflicting as to be confusing rather than helpful. Surveys in Europe and the United States have found that whilst the most common method is a variation of salary and commission combined, there is also extensive use of salary only and commission only. Moreover, there is no clear evidence of relative effectiveness of the methods. The surveys show very little correlation between any method and measures of corporate success such as sales growth or profitability. Further, any payment method with a high proportion of commission presents the problem of deciding the basis for the commission. There have been cases where a misjudged rate that could not be changed has resulted in some salesmen being paid more than the Managing Director. More usually, the rate is not fixed for all time, and many salesmen suspect that if they exceed their targets the commission formula will be changed so that next year they will have to work even harder to maintain their income.

Regardless of the research findings, many sales managers remain unconvinced about any method of payment that does not incorporate a major element of commission.

However, for a company seeking a payment method, the wide variety of methods used do at least provide a comprehensive range of options from which to select.

6. Selecting a Payments Method – Objectives

The company should first decide the objectives it requires its sales force to achieve. This is the basis not only of a payment method but also job specification and sales force size and structure. Possible objectives are one or more of the following:
(a) maximise sales
(b) maximise profit
(c) advise/inform customers
(d) provide service
(e) assist in brand image creation
(f) develop contacts
(g) gather information
(h) increase market penetration.

The objectives likely to be important to the company will depend on the nature of the purchase decision process and the company's marketing strategy.

The purchase decision process determines the range of activities that the sales force must perform. For example, purchasers of a technological product such as a word processor or microcomputer will require information, advice, guidance and service. The salesman's task therefore will be extended, requiring a great deal of the time and patience. In such circumstances, payment entirely or mainly by commission on sales is unlikely to produce the attitude and behaviour that is necessary for salesmen to make sales.

In contrast, if the purchase is simple – a straight 're-buy' or repeat of a frequently made purchase, such as the purchase of stationery by an office manager – then commission might well be a good motivator towards a high call rate and a persistent sales approach. A high commission element or even commission-only payment is often used in the sales of products which are strictly inessential, but which represent significant purchases, in terms of seriousness (life assurance, encyclopaedia) or cost (double glazing). It should be noted, however, that salesmen and the selling of such products are generally of low status and synonymous with high-pressure selling and other undesirable practices.

The company's marketing strategy, especially the 'sales load' to be taken by personal selling is the other major factor influencing decisions about the sales force, including method of payment. For example, a 'pull' strategy, relying on heavy consumer advertising to bring consumers into retailers requires salesmen to play a servicing role, ensuring that the product is stocked and promoted. In contrast, a 'push' strategy places emphasis on selling into retailers, and thus offers much greater opportunities for salesmen to influence sales and is thus more suited to a commission system of payment. This is an additional rationale for the high commission levels of life assurance selling where it is left to the financially motivated salesman to exploit the sales opportunities.

7. Conclusion

Tradition appears to be a major reason for the phenomenon of paying salesmen according to the level of sales achieved. There is some case for treating the remuneration of salesmen differently, as so much of their work cannot be supervised in the way possible with office staff. However, it should be asked why typists are not paid according to the number of letters they type, or telephonists according to the number of calls they make and why, indeed, teachers are not paid according to the examination success of their students.

While the evidence on the effectiveness of commission payments is conflicting, the method does have some intuitive appeal for use in one of its variations in at least some circumstances.

A company considering a payment method for salesmen

should observe the range of methods in use and decide on the basis of what is most compatible with its objectives and circumstances.

Answer 46   **Industrial and**   Question page 10
                  Organisational Buying

---

1. Industrial Markets and Organisational Markets

Industrial marketing is among the more neglected areas of marketing study, considered either less important or less exciting than topics concerned primarily with consumers. This neglect is certainly not justified in terms of relative turnover, as industrial sales are at least equal to sales to consumers.

Although the term 'industrial market' is often used to cover all non-consumer markets, a more comprehensive title is 'organisational markets', of which industrial is one of three subsets, as shown below.

(a) *Producer / manufacturer*: Companies and organisations in the public and private sectors who buy (or rent) goods and services to be used in the production of other goods and services.

(b) *Reseller markets*: Retailers, wholesalers and agents, buying for resale.

(c) *Government markets*: Government departments (at national and local levels) buying (or renting) the goods and services required for carrying out the business of government.

These three market types are very similar as far as marketing is concerned, and although throughout this answer the term 'industrial' marketing is used almost exclusively, the points made apply equally to reseller and government markets.

Consumer markets can be defined as individuals and households who buy or rent goods and services for personal consumption.

2. Organisational Markets and Consumer Markets

The differences between the two markets derive partly from the goods and services bought and partly from the buyers.

Although many goods, such as machine tools, fork-lift trucks and chemicals are bought only by organisations, others, such as telephone and bank services, cars and pencils are bought by both organisations and consumers. It should be noted however, that organisations generally buy in larger quantities and more directly than from the retail outlets normally used by consumers.

It is at the level of the buyers involved that the major differences between industrial and consumer markets occurs.

3. The Number of Buyers

Whilst consumer markets can consist of millions of buyers, many industrial markets number only tens or hundreds. This has implications for promotion, which has to be targeted accurately, and for market research which uses small samples and secondary data sources.

4. Group Buying

This is a feature of industrial markets. Some consumer purchases are decided by groups, in the form of the family or a part of the family. Consumer durables purchases, such as cars and furniture normally depend on the views of the entire family, and even more frequent purchases, such as food, although apparently made by the housewife alone, are influenced by the tastes and preferences of other family members.

In industrial markets, group buying affects a much greater proportion of purchases and is much stronger as it is necessary to meet the criteria of a number of interest groups within the organisation. For example, the purchase of a fork-lift truck might be initiated by a work study engineer, progressed by the warehouse manager and influenced by the transport manager, accountant, personnel manager, and trade union representative before the order is placed by the purchasing manager.

The number and seniority of organisation members participating depends on the type of purchase and type of company. For significant purchases, involving a large investment or an aspect of company policy, a company director or even the entire board might be involved. A purchase primarily concerning production will be heavily influenced by production and engineering specialists whereas office equipment buying will be more influenced by the office manager and the accountant. The distribution of influence in general varies between organisations according to the nature of the business and the established power of various departments. For example, in a toiletries company, the marketing department is likely to have a dominant influence on all operations, including purchasing, whereas engineers would be expected to be more influential in a machine-tools company.

The implication of group purchase decision making for companies selling to industrial markets is that it is essential to identify the decision makers involved and to ensure that appropriate communication and sales effort is directed towards them.

5. Buying Goals

It is often claimed that the major difference between consumer and industrial marketing is that the former is subject to irrational buying, whereas in the latter, buying decisions are reached rationally. Unfortunately, 'rationality' in the sense used in economics is not a very helpful concept when applied to marketing.

Provided that a consumer seeks to maximise his utility, i.e. his purchasing behaviour is consistent with his objectives, he can be said to be acting rationally. Thus, it could be argued that a status-concious man buying a Jaguar because he believes that it will enhance his prestige is acting quite rationally provided that he does perceive this effect following his purchase. Another man buying a Metro because of its low purchase cost and economy might be acting no more rationally. What would be irrational would be for the prestige-seeker to buy a Metro.

When applied to consumer behaviour, rationality is generally taken to mean the systematic and considered selection of the product that best performs functional tasks at minimum cost, rather than the impulsive purchase of a product on the basis of attributes such as cosmetic design, packaging, branding and advertising.

6. Rationalty in Industrial Buying

Whether or not some or all consumer buying is irrational in the way described, industrial buyers cerainly have the motivation and opportunity to purchase rationally.

First, the products and services bought are normally

functional and do not have the status and prestige associations of many consumer purchases. Second, there is often a great deal at stake. A component bought at a lower price can accumulate considerable savings and increase profits. Conversely, a component that is unreliable or delivered late can cause reduced production and financial loss. Third, in industrial markets, not only are such gains and losses larger than in consumer purchases but also they are more subject to quantification by means of research and value analysis. While it is very difficult (and probably not worthwhile) for a housewife to make an objective comparison between washing-up liquids, a company would find it both possible and profitable to determine cost savings on products bought for frequent use.

The implication here for companies selling to industrial markets is the need to ascertain and meet the requirements of industrial purchases – price, delivery, reliability and so on.

7. Irrationality in Industrial Buying

It has been noted that not all industrial buying is completely rational all the time. After all, the rational industrial buyers are the same people who are irrational consumers outside work. Industrial buyers vary in their knowledge, experience and attitude to risk. For example, some might wish to maintain a safe profile by purchasing from established suppliers rather than investigating and risking lower-priced but unknown sources. Similarly, there might be a purely personal preference to buy from certain companies or salesmen.

These various aspects of the purchase have been described as 'task' elements, concerned with the product's specification and suitability for the purchase; and 'non-task' elements, concerned with personal factors such as the buyer's risk-avoidance and preference for certain sales approaches.

The implication here is clearly the need to research organisations and buyers.

8. Conclusion

Industrial markets (and other forms of organisational markets) have certain distinguishing characteristics, principally related to the buyers and the buying process. While the basic tasks for industrial marketers are much the same as for consumer marketers – the identification and satisfaction of needs and wants – industrial markets do require a modification of emphasis and approach.

| Answer 47 | Standardisation in International Marketing | Question page 10 |

1. International and Single-country Marketing

The question of whether international marketing is different from domestic or single-country marketing is illustrated by the contrasting 'Behaviourist' and 'Environmentalist' approaches.

Behaviourists take a 'global village' view that individual wants, motives and behaviour are the same throughout the world, as demonstrated by Coronation Street being shown on Turkish television and the international success of pop groups.

Environmentalists claim that as factors such as demography, economics and culture vary so much throughout the world, standardised marketing is impossible.

2. International Marketing

Selling in various national markets, whether done by exporting or the use of multi-national companies, is distinguished from single-company operations by the barriers of distance, documentation and difference. Whilst these barriers can be more imaginary than real they do present obstacles, especially to companies new to international marketing.

The distance to overseas markets can be less than to destinations within the home country. The impression of distance is often reinforced by additional documentation requirements. Even within a trading bloc such as the Common Market there is more paperwork than for domestic marketing. There is also the additional administration and risk of currency dealings.

The barrier that most affects marketing is that of difference. Such differences can be classified as:

(a) economic
(b) cultural
(c) marketing

178

(d) climatic/geographical
(e) political/legal.

3. Economic Differences

Income and industrial structure are a major influence on the goods and services that a country needs and can buy.

Average national income obviously affects the ability to purchase, but also important is the distribution of this income, as some countries contain extreme socio-economic segmentation. This applies not only to Third World countries but also to a lesser extent to more affluent countries such as the United Kingdom and United States where, despite high unemployment, those in jobs have maintained a high standard of living.

A country's industrial structure – agrarian, raw-material producing, industrialised and so on influences the types of goods demanded.

4. Cultural

Whereas the amount that consumers have to spend depends on economic factors, the way in which they choose to spend is determined by lifestyles and values. This implies much more than the need to use the local language, as literal translations are sometimes not appropriate. For example, in Germany the Austin Maestro computer uses a male voice, as German drivers would not be happy with receiving motoring information and instructions from a woman. Similarly, the British habit of high television viewing led to high sales of video-recorders. In Switzerland there is a dislike of artificial fibres and a preference for articles, especially clothing, made from wool. In France, chocolate is used in cooking, whereas in Italy it is served between slices of bread as a children's snack.

5. Marketing

A company's range of decisions in some countries is constrained by local market factors, particularly distribution and advertising media. The Hypermarche in France, the Verbrauchemarkt in Germany and the relative absence of CTN-type outlets in these countries offers both opportunities and problems for confectionery companies. The structure of advertising media in most European countries offers much less television advertising than is available in Britain and the United States, which requires modification to any television-based marketing strategies.

6. Climate/Geography
For a very wide range of products these factors can require considerable modification or even prevent marketing at all. For example, the problems with the marketing of chocolate increase with the temperature and in hot countries the product is sold from refrigerated cabinets. Cars require special cooling systems in hot countries and anti-corrosion treatment in cold countries where roads are salted frequently. Similarly, soft drinks might be sold as smart or refreshing in temperate climates and as thirst-quenching in areas of hot weather.

7. Political/Legal
Harmonisation of the laws relating to business is seen as such a major help to international business that it has been adopted as a prime objective by the European Economic Community. Elsewhere however, companies find different requirements on product safety, packaging, car exhaust emission and advertising. Even within the EEC there are differences, such as in Germany the prohibition of comparison advertising and in France restrictions on the portrayal of women.

8. Marketing's Response to Differences Between National Markets
While there are numerous examples, such as those given above, of differences between national markets it is quite easy to find cases where a single marketing strategy has been successful in many countries, for example, McDonalds, the Austin Mini and Coca Cola. A company considering entry to a new country should use market research in much the same way as it would when developing a new product in its domestic market. The objectives of such research should be to ascertain market size (if any) and the nature of any modifications required to meet the local conditions covered in sections 3–7.

The company can then decide its marketing mix. A much-quoted framework for this exercise is that of Keegan.[1]

1. Warren J. Keegan 'Multi-national product planning: Strategic alternatives'. Journal of Marketing January 1969.

Straight extension
The introduction of the product in the same form and with the same promotion as at home. As already noted, this strategy has been successful for McDonalds and Coca Cola.

Communication adaptation
The use of an unchanged product but with promotion modified to meet cultural or legal factors. For example, in Germany, the Maxwell House slogan 'The great American coffee' had to be changed when it was found that Germans do not rate American coffee highly.

Product adaptation
Using the same promotion, but altering the product. For example, in France, Marks and Spencer had to offer changing rooms and clothes in different colours.

Dual adaptation
Changing both product and promotion. This has been done with certain cosmetics, where different markets require not only different fragrances, but also respond to different advertising appeals.

Product innovation and Communication innovation
Designing a new product (and consequently a new promotion) to meet a demand in another country. For example, Honda produced domestic lawn mowers specially for the European market. This strategy is the most difficult and carries the most risk and, for once, it is not clear that Honda have been successful with their innovation.

9. Conclusion

It is not possible to generalise about the feasibility of standardisation in international marketing. What works for some products in some markets does not work for all.

Standardisation offers economies, as the costs of product development, manufacture, packaging and advertising are spread over larger sales revenue. In addition, a uniform image is presented, the cost of personnel training is minimised and centralised control is maximised. However, there are limits to standardisation which should be ascertained and monitored by market reaearch.

Many markets differ so little that standardisation, or something quite like it can be used. Although the roads and climate of Asia and Africa might require special cars, minimal modification is needed for most European countries and North America. For example, the Volkswagon Golf was renamed the Rabbit in the United States and the Fiat Ritmo became the Strada in Britain, and different advertising campaigns were used. However, these are marginal alterations in terms of the investment required to produce completely new cars.

To some extent international markets should be considered as market segments whose response characteristics must be researched and met.

Answer 48 **Entering Overseas Markets** Question page 11

1. The International Marketing Decision

What was once the opportunity to operate in a number of national markets is now becoming a necessity for many companies if they are to achieve the sales levels necessary to fund growth. The decision is now about the means by which to organise the international involvement.

One extreme is the *multinational* operation of companies such as Beecham, Ford and Nestlé, who organise not only Marketing but also production, regardless of national boundaries. The other extreme, the export of finished products from the home country, is clearly much more practical for the company under review.

International marketing requires a company to take decisions on
(a) the strategy to adopt
(b) the markets to enter
(c) the marketing mixes to offer.

2. Strategy

This initial stage involves defining objectives and policies in relation to international marketing. First, the company should decide the proportion of sales it intends to obtain abroad. The domestic market might be maintained as the major part of the business with overseas sales limited to product lines where production capacity is too great to be absorbed by the domestic market alone. Alternatively, the plan might be to develop large overseas sales which will move the company towards multinational status. It should be noted, however, that regardless of the level at which international sales are set, it is essential to supply the market promptly and consistently.

3. The Markets to Enter

The company must also decide the number and types of market to enter. As a medium-sized company new to international marketing, it would be sensible to concentrate resources on developing relatively few markets, possibly only one, and gain knowledge and experience that can be used to improve performance elsewhere at a later time.

The types of markets most suitable to enter will depend on the characteristics of the company and its products. Again, in view of the company's inexperience internationally, the most suitable markets are likely to be those which are closest, have the greatest similarity to the domestic market and have the minimum requirements for documentation. Thus, EEC and/or Commonwealth countries are often the markets to which British companies sell first.

4. Appraising Markets

Potential overseas markets should be appraised by a process similar to that used for new products in the domestic market. It is necessary to analyse present and future demand, competition, legal constraints and currency rates to arrive at an estimate of return on capital.

Relevant information is available from government departments and banks (both at home and in the countries under review). Without criticising such sources unfairly, it must be pointed out that they cannot be expected to be experts on every market. Therefore, it might be necessary to complement this information with a survey conducted specifically by a market research agency. Such a survey can use published sources or limited primary research, and consequently need not be as expensive as might be thought. Accurate, low-cost market information is often available from a local advertising agency.

In any case, whereas it is always as important to control

research expenditure as any other, research funds are well invested if the information obtained assists in assessing the markets and avoiding costly mistakes.

International marketing is likely to involve greater costs and more risks than marketing at home. These include extra transport, insurance, translations and currency fluctuations, in addition to any product redesign or repackaging required by local demand or regulations. It is essential that such costs are not overlooked when making the return-on-investment calculations.

5. The Marketing Mixes to Offer
The simplest way for the toy company to become involved in international marketing is to sell some of its present output abroad. This can be achieved with the minimum change in product design, packaging, organisation and investment by a 'straight extension' overseas of the current marketing mix. Alternatively, depending on the market research data, it might be necessary to modify the marketing mix by redesigning the product, the promotion or both.

6. Means of Market Entry
Having determined which countries offer profitable opportunities and the marketing mixes to offer, the company must decide the best means of market entry. The three major options are:
(a) exporting
(b) joint-venturing
(c) direct investment.

7. Exporting
Exporting can be *indirect* or *direct*:

Indirect exporting is the use of independent international marketing middlemen. Such a middleman is based or has an office in Britain and has knowledge of the export markets. The service offered can vary. Some act as no more than agents and do little more than respond to enquiries from customers and pass on orders. Others undertake all documentation, place large orders for their own stock and are active in distributing and promoting the product, obtaining market information and giving advice on marketing tactics.

Direct exporting involves selling into the overseas markets. The simplest method is to use foreign-based distributors or agents who sell on behalf of the toy company within a given territory, usually an entire country. As with the middlemen used in indirect exporting, the range of service offered can vary.

A more developed form of direct exporting is to employ salesmen to travel the overseas territories and obtain orders from wholesalers or retailers. As business increases, this can evolve into an export department or division.

If sales are expected to be high, the company can establish, in addition to or instead of the export department, overseas sales branches or subsidiaries. Such an office allows the manufacturer to achieve greater presence and control in the market. It can handle warehousing, distribution and promotion and be used as a centre for display and customer service. Overseas branches can be established for a country or group or countries.

8. Joint-venturing

Joint-venturing requires more commitment and investment than exporting and can take a number of forms. The company can *licence* or subcontract the right to a manufacturing process, trademark or recipe to a local company for a fee or royalty, as is done throughout the world by Coca Cola. Alternatively, the company can retain the marketing function and *subcontract manufacturing* locally. This is done by some tyre companies. It might suit a company to supply management expertise to a local company which supplies manufacturing capacity and distribution under a *management contracting* agreement. Lastly the company can form with a local company in *joint ownership* and control of manufacturing and marketing.

9. Direct Investment

The ultimate form of involvement is the establishment of local assembly or manufacturing facilities. As this type of operation extends to other countries, the company moves towards the multinational status described in Section 1.

10. Recommendations for the Toy Company

In view of the company's size and complete inexperience in international marketing, it would be well advised to proceed cautiously and minimise its investment and risk while testing the market.

In order to do this testing however, it is necessary to spend at certain minimum levels. For example, use of a low-service agent might require only low outlays but is also likely to bring low standards of attention. Consequently, apparent failure in the market might be caused by inadequate marketing support rather than inadequacies in the product.

Therefore, having researched a suitable market, the company should apply at least the level of marketing effort that it would consider necessary in the home market. The investment and risk can be minimised by concentrating on one country or part of a country.

International marketing does not involve any principles not found in domestic marketing. However, because of the risk and uncertainty in dealing with unknown markets it is probably necessary to use greater care and attention.

Answer 49   **Consumerism**   Question page 11

1. Introduction

The short answer to this question is 'Yes, in some cases'. However, in order to give a more complete answer and, more important, to investigate the implications for marketing management, it is necessary to examine the nature and causes of consumerism.

In many countries during the last two decades there have been developments with titles such as 'consumer protection', 'consumerism' and 'social pressure groups'.

Consumer protection is the collection of laws, regulations, codes and information set up by government, industry and consumer groups to strengthen consumers' power in the market place.

Consumerism is the part played in this process by organised groups of consumers. Consumerism is not the only example of individuals grouped together to bring pressure to bear on companies, but it is the only one that is concerned exclusively with matters relating to the purchase and use of products and services.

Social pressure groups include; environmentalists who, for example, are concerned with the effect of marketing inasmuch as advertising posters and billboards affect the appearance of towns and the countryside, with additives to products and with the litter caused by discarded packaging; and feminist groups who attack sexism in advertising.

2. The Scope of Consumerism

Consumerism is concerned with consumer welfare in terms of both rights and information and also the choice and prices of goods available.

Thus consumerism covers:
(a) Accuracy and truth in advertising and packaging.
(b) The safety and durability of products.
(c) The effects on prices and choice of mergers, acquisitions and the existence of barriers to market entry.
(d) The effects on prices of advertising expenditure.

Consumerism has been organised successfully in many countries, an example of which is the Consumers' Association in Britain, which has around half a million members. There is a case for regarding government departments such as the Ministry for Consumer Affairs and the Office of Fair Trading as part of the consumerism movement but these and the local government Trading Standards Inspectorate are probably best described as parts of the machinery of consumer protection. Consumerism by its nature has independent and pressure-group status.

3. The Rationale of Consumer Protection

The basic tenet of consumerism is that consumers are at a disadvantage when purchasing and therefore need advice and protection. The consumer is seen as inexperienced, unorganised, inexpert, timorous and unaware of the law and his or her rights. He or she is easily outwitted or intimidated by confident, experienced companies and their legal advisers.

Therefore, the doctrine of *caveat emptor* is unlikely to provide adequate consumer protection and consumerism defines the rights of buyers to include:

(a) Complete information on product contents, ingredients and methods of manufacture.
(b) Protection against defective and shoddy products.
(c) Protection against misleading advertising and high-pressure personal selling.
(d) Recompense, restitution and damages.

Moreover, all these rights should be enforceable quickly, easily and at low cost with support from the criminal code, if appropriate.

4. Consumerism and the Marketing Concept

At first sight, the emergence and development of consumerism is paradoxical in the context of the marketing concept. The explanation lies in the fundamental and inevitable conflict between the objectives of consumers and those of companies. Consumers seek very good products at very low prices, whereas companies seek the highest prices and the lowest costs in order to maximise profit.

The response of companies is to reduce costs through increased efficiency and economies of scale, and to incorporate low-cost design into products. To that extent this is a legitimate and logical implementation of market segmentation. Not all consumers will buy the quality of a Rolls-Royce or Rover, and for these segments there are Fords and Volkswagens.

The divergence between consumerism and some companies' version of the marketing concept comes at the point when costs are pushed down to the level that the product becomes shoddy, or when advertising is used to mislead consumers about quality, performance or price.

In other cases, failure to implement the marketing concept is due simply to companies' not being aware of changes in consumer demand. An example of this is the loss of market by American car manufacturers. Leaving aside differences in production methods, a major cause of the success of Nissan, Toyota and the others is that they have produced cars of the type and reliability that consumers wanted and which were not available from the home companies.

5. Consumerism and Marketing Policy

There is understandable concern that increased standards of quality and information will raise costs and reduce sales.

Some companies are worried that they will lose competitiveness by unilaterally meeting the requirements of consumerism. The outcome of this belief is to wait for the Government to set legal standards or a trade association to set industry standards before modifying practice.

On examination it can be seen that consumerism does no more than represent a change of emphasis in the demand of large groups of consumers and that within the marketing concept it is essential for companies to respond. Consumerism should be seen as a source of valuable and low-cost market research for analysis and incorporation into marketing plans.

Marks and Spencer and Sainsburys have been successful with a policy of consistently high quality, and in the case of Marks and Spencer the routine exchange of goods and refunds. Many German and Japanese companies have made quality, reliability and service a major part of their marketing mixes. Car manufacturers from all countries are giving extended guarantees against mechanical failure and corrosion. Although the major British brewers initially considered the Campaign for Real Ale a nuisance, they later realised that there were profits to be made by meeting demand from this vociferous and sizeable market segment.

6. Consumerism and Marketing Management

Some companies, expecially in the United States, reacted to consumerism by establishing 'Consumer Affairs Departments' to deal with consumer complaints and other feedback and to represent consumerist issues within the company. Whilst this indicates recognition of the importance of consumerism, there is a danger that the company considers that the issue is dealt with simply by establishing the department. In fact, the implications of consumerism, like those of marketing, must run right through the company and become part of a philosophy that permeates every decision.

Nonetheless, it is important to keep consumerism in perspective. While it is a significant force, it does not always represent all consumers in a market. As mentioned above, the major brewers produced (or rediscovered) cask-conditioned ales in response to CAMRA. However, they realised that their major markets were still with lager and other pressurised beers, ciders, spirits and so on.

Although consumerism is an important consideration in marketing decision making, it should not become another marketing fad, hailed as the answer to all problems and to which all activity and development must be subordinated.

Question 50	Consumer Protection	Question page 11

1. Consumer Protection

There is some dispute about what constitutes consumer protection and even more dispute about the amount of consumer protection that is desirable socially and economically.

At one extreme, consumers are expected to protect themselves − the doctrine of *caveat emptor*. A slightly less *laissez-faire* approach is to educate consumers so that they are better able to protect themselves, by providing literature and advice centres. Further stages are to prohibit misleading information and to require the disclosure of certain information.

More rigorous protection is to require products to reach certain standards and for companies to be liable if they do not. The most stringent forms of protection involve the control of prices, competition and mergers and the prohibition of certain products.

In Britain there are examples from all of these philosophies, and consumer protection covers the following areas.
(a) The performance and safety of products.
(b) The disclosure and accuracy of information in terms of weight, dimension, content and performance.
(c) The quality and content of food and drink.
(d) The availability and promotion of certain products.
(e) The disclosure of information relating to credit and hire purchase.
(f) The morality of advertising.
(g) The security of money paid for certain products and services.
(h) The effect of restrictive trade practices.

2. Codification of Consumer Protection

In Britain, consumer protection is a complicated collection of statutory and voluntary controls. Whereas in certain countries, notably Germany and Sweden, there is a single consolidated system, in Britain consumer protection is contained in a range of civil and criminal law, agreements between industries and government and within industries.

Thus the scope and effect of consumer protection is potentially confusing for both consumers and companies. Although some elements affect all transactions, the great proportion are very important to some types of business but largely irrelevant to others. For example, a food company would be very concerned with the Food and Drug Acts, but unaffected by the laws on consumer credit.

Moreover, the laws for Scotland are not the same as for the rest of Britain.

3. Civil Law

Under civil law, consumers are protected in every purchase by the law of contract, as laid down by the Sale of Goods Acts 1893 and 1979, the Supply of Goods (Implied Terms) Act 1973, the Unfair Contract Terms Act 1977 and the supply of Goods and Services Act, 1982. The contract of sale requires that the goods are of 'merchantable quality', or 'fit for the purpose' for which bought. In other words a cooker must cook, glue must stick. The 1973 and 1977 Acts prevents traders from avoiding their liabilities by the use of exclusion clauses.

Consumers can proceed, usually for restitution or damages, through the County Court or High Court. The Small Claims Court provides consumers with facilities for quick and inexpensive resolution of disputes involving not more than £500. There is disagreement about the effectiveness of civil law as a means of consumer protection, as so much depends on the financial resources, knowledge and persistence of individual consumers.

4. Criminal Law

The range of consumer protection available under the criminal code is diverse and complex. The British Code of Advertising Practice refers to over eighty statutes and statutory instruments relating to advertising alone.

The Acts that are best known and which have the widest effect are the Fair Trading Act 1973 and the Trade Descriptions Acts 1968 and 1972.

The Fair Trading Act established the post of Director-

General of Fair Trading and an organisation to oversee trading matters relating to consumer interests. Among the results have been a number of 'orders' strengthening consumer rights.

Under the Trade Descriptions Acts, it is an offence:

(a) to apply a false trade description to any goods or services, or

(b) to supply or offer to supply any goods or services to which a false trade description is applied.

The Acts have affected all copywriting on advertising, packaging and display that make factual statements. However, statements that are very general, or based on opinion, such as 'The best lager in the world', and 'Extra value', are permitted, on the grounds that such opinions can legitimately differ.

Accurate disclosure of quantities, weights, dimensions and other factual data is required under the Weights and Measures Acts 1963, 1976 and 1979. This legislation affects the marketing of a very wide range of products such as food, toiletries, decorating materials and stationery.

The Food and Drug Act 1955 regulates the production, handling, preparation, description, condition and sale of food and is of very great relevance to any company involved in food and catering.

Under the Consumer Credit Act 1974 and the various regulations that have been made subsequently, there are complicated requirements for the disclosure of information in advertisements and display material. The topics covered include creditors, the cash price of goods, the APR (annual percentage rate of charge), minimum deposits, security and status requirements, amount and frequency of payment, and so on and so on. Protection is given against 'extortionate' rates of interest.

Consumers also have extensive rights relating to entering credit and hire purchase agreements, and all companies concerned with the provision of credit have to be licensed by the Director-General of Fair Trading. The result is a very complex system of requirements for all companies concerned with credit and hire purchase.

5. Advertising Regulation

In addition to the law, there is consumer protection under industry codes and voluntary agreements.

This applies particularly to advertising where the Independent Broadcasting Authority (IBA) controls advertising on television and radio, and The Advertising Standards Authority (ASA) controls all other advertising.

The closest regulation is on television where certain products, chiefly cigarettes, are banned completely, and all advertisements require approval before transmission. Both the IBA and ASA have Codes of Practice to which advertisements must conform. These codes cover advertising in general and in particular certain sensitive areas such as alcohol, tobacco, and treatments for slimming and hair loss.

Apart from the requirement to be 'honest, truthful and legal', advertisements must also be 'decent'. For example, advertisements must not be offensive, encourage anti-social or dangerous behaviour by children or play on fears or superstitions.

As noted above, television and radio advertisements must conform to the IBA Code before transmission. Advertisements in other media which are found to be in breach of the ASA Code have to be withdrawn immediately.

Tobacco is further regulated by an agreement between the industry and government in respect of product type, advertising levels and media and packaging – the health warning on packets.

6. Trade Association Agreements and Codes

Many trade associations require members to conform to agreed standards of conduct. Failure to do so usually results in refusal or withdrawal of membership, which in turn reduces the company's attractiveness to consumers.

7. Conclusion

Consumer protection is a major issue for marketing management in Britain, if for no other reason because its diffuse and complex nature makes comprehension extremely difficult.

In addition, in many cases, for example Consumer Credit, the restrictions and requirements are not only complex but also extensive.

With so many laws and codes affecting different aspects of the product, advertising, packaging, display and credit arrangements, consumer protection is certainly a major issue.

Failure to meet the legal and other requirements can result in considerable damages, awards, fines, bad publicity and loss of trade association membership.

However, the laws and codes relating to consumer protection should not be considered only as a problem. Often the standards made necessary by consumer protection are advantageous to well-managed and socially responsible companies as they increase consumer confidence and force less scrupulous companies to take on the costs and effort required to maintain high standards of social responsibility.

Appendix 1

The Use of Case Studies

Case studies are used both for teaching and examinations. For teaching, they allow students to develop their skills not only at marketing but also at analysis. For examinations (where their use is becoming increasingly popular), cases help to assess students' comprehension of marketing and their ability to apply this to problems that represent, as closely as possible, actual marketing situations. Cases vary in length between one and several pages and deal with both specific topics – sales management, new product development, pricing and so on – and general marketing policy and action. With the specific-topic type of case, the student has the advantage of a clear indication of the problem under review, whereas with general cases often the main problem is to find the problem.

For this reason it is an example of the general case that is given here, with a suggested solution and, possibly more important, a suggested method for tackling such case studies.

General Points Concerning the Solution of Case Studies

Certain 'open-book' or untimed examinations, or examinations where case studies are distributed in advance, invite students to obtain more information relevant to the case. Otherwise, cases usually contain all the information necessary for solution. Where further information is available, it is essential to use only what is relevant. When unsure about a marketing problem (either a case or in reality) there is a temptation to seek illumination from more data or research, rather than from more concentrated analysis of the information already available. This is particularly true of the Bradflax case which, despite brevity, contains quite enough for both analysis and recommendations.

Sometimes it is necessary or useful to make assumptions about some aspect of the case. Whilst students cannot be expected to be experts in the area covered by the case, it is desirable that such assumptions are consistent with real conditions; for example, that the health-food market is expanding or that children are the main consumers of baked beans. It is important that assumptions are clearly stated and followed throughout the answer.

The information given is often not in a coherent or sequential form. Whether or not this is deliberate it is quite valid, as this is the form in which information is presented and obtained from companies. If a company could enunciate the problem, it would probably have solved or even prevented it.

Remember that there is no uniquely correct course of marketing action, either in cases or real marketing situations. Plans are capable of infinite variation concerning the amounts of money to spend, the design of products, the advertising campaign and its elements, and so on. In addition, the unpredictability of the response of consumers, competition and other environmental factors makes it necessary to make broad assumptions. Thus there are always choices of objectives and of the means of achieving them. But just as there is more than one 'right' answer, there are answers that are wrong, such as for example advertising to farmers during the break in Coronation Street, setting a penetration price for an exclusive perfume or omitting to test market a new brand of detergent.

An approach to the Solution of Case Studies
It is important to approach cases systematically, and the use of a framework such as the following is recommended for the general, marketing policy case.

1. Analyse the company, its present position and possible future position
(a) *The company's market*: who are the consumers and what, where and why they buy.
(b) *The company's capabilities*: its resources, products and image.
(c) *The competition's capabilities*.

(d) *The company environment*: the factors that affect its present and future options.

2. *Develop marketing strategy*

The market to enter, the products to develop and discontinue.

3. *Develop marketing tactics*

The marketing mixes to offer.

The second and third stages of case study solution are based on the first stage. It is essential to carry out the analysis first, as students are often tempted to jump straight to the later stages and suggest for example large advertising campaigns which, by reference to the analysis of the company's finances and markets, are seen to be impossible and unnecessary. It is also important that the recommendations are as fundamental as considered necessary. For example, if it really seems that the company should close down and reinvest its money – say so.

The Bradflax case – The Bradford Flax Carpet Company

The Company

The Bradford Flax Carpet Company Limited makes flax carpets. Sales had risen from less than £$\frac{1}{2}$ million in 1963 to over £10 million by 1975. However, after this date sales had slowed and by 1982 were £12 million, a considerable decline in volume terms. Profit had been around 15% of sales in the early period, but this had become a slight loss by 1982.

The Market

The Bradford Flax sales department were at a loss to explain the decline. They pointed out that the product was 30% cheaper than wool and nylon carpets and that a competitive flax carpet, Kingsaki Smoothflax was selling well.

Market Research

An attitudinal market research study conducted by a London agency for the company had produced a range of negative comments, of which the following are typical.

'They're alright if you just want cheap carpets'

'There is little call for flax carpets nowadays'

'Flax carpets make such a mess – customers complain about the little bits that come out of them' (from a carpet store manager)

'Flax carpets are rather dull – real carpets have much better colours and designs'

'They're alright if you're some kind of masochist – if you like having your feet scratched'

'Bradflax – is that some kind of electric cable?'

'Flax carpets – never heard of them'.

Posing as customers, Bradford Flax employees had visited 30 Bradflax stockists, only five of which had spontaneously offered Bradflax when asked about carpets.

Sales Promotion

At many stockists there was a Kingsaki display containing a leaflet which made the following points:

1. Smoothflax carpets wear well – nearly one-third of our sales go to offices, shops and hospitals.

2. Smoothflax carpets are *smooth* – most of our domestic sales are for use in bedrooms.

3. Smoothflax carpets improve with wear – as the surplus weft strands disappear, your carpet takes on a deep lustrous tone.

Advise the Bradford Flax Carpet Company on the marketing action that it should take.

A Solution to the Bradflax case

  1 Analysis

(a) *The company's market*: Can be segmented into industrial and consumer buyers.

    Industrial buyers can be further segmented on the lines of offices, hospitals and schools. It is necessary to identify.

- *who* influences the buying decision, e.g. architects, surveyors, hospitals administrators.
- *when* buying decisions are made
- *the buying objectives* e.g. hard wear, low cost, delivery.

    Consumer markets must be similarly analysed in terms of:

- *buyer characteristics*: e.g. age, socio-economic grade, sex
- *benefits sought*: e.g. cost, durability stain-resistance, colour pattern, texture
- *timing of purchase*: moving, house/flat, season, frequency.
- *reasons for purchase*: moving, redecorating, previous carpet worn out

- *outlet used*: furniture store, discount warehouse, department store
- *influences on purchase*: advertising, social contacts, salesmen.

Currently, the company appears to be selling only in the consumer market.

(b) *The company's capabilities*: Its ability to make, develop and market products; its distribution system; the possibilities for alternative use of its land and capital assets.

At present, it appears that the company's products are not attractive to consumers and that it is getting poor support from the distribution system.

(c) *The competition's capabilities*: The number, size, sales levels, market shares, product range, prices and quality of competitive companies. Bradflax's price advantage over wool and synthetic carpets appears to be interpreted as a sign of inferiority, although a similar, competitive product seems to be successful.

(d) *The company's environment*: Is it possible that increased living standards have made lower-priced carpets less necessary? Or has improved technology in other carpet materials eroded competitive advantage?

2 *Strategy*

(a) *General comments*: The company's £12 million sales represent considerable revenue, although no doubt lower than would have been achieved with good progress. It must be decided if the company has the capability to use this sales base to return to profitability. If not, the company could consider converting its assets by redeveloping the property for housing, as a theme park or for some other purpose quite different from carpet manufacture. Assuming such a revolutionary change to be unnecessary (or more likely unacceptable to the directors), various options based on the company's current activities can be considered.

Note: before any marketing changes it is essential to examine the company's costs as it could be that drift in this area has contributed to the fall in profits. It is quite possible that increased sales revenue could lead to no increase in profit, or even to a loss.

(b) *Organisation*: The company might need to consider the

appointment of a marketing manager, if not the establishment of a marketing department.

(c) *Markets to enter*: The industrial market seems attractive, provided that the company can meet the specifications; research would be necessary to ascertain market structure, requirements and buying patterns. The consumer market should be maintained, as it is here that the company appears to be currently obtaining its sales revenue. The objective is to make the alterations in the marketing mix necessary for success.

(d) *New products/new markets*: The company might extend its range, either by manufacture or buying in. The present machinery might be capable of making products such as mats, fabrics and wall coverings. An alternative way to extend the range is by the method increasingly popular with British companies – the distribution of imported products. Lastly, the company could sell its existing products through new channels; making for own-branding or for a catalogue company might be attractive, in view of the company's inexperience at marketing.

3 Tactics

(a) *General comments*: Assume that the strategy decided is:
- to improve performance in consumer markets
- to enter industrial markets
- to develop new products.

The company should take care to avoid the overcommitment that could be caused by attempting to proceed on all these fronts at once. It would seem best to build on the existing consumer markets and seek to extend this activity to selected industrial markets before starting on the complex and risky process of developing new products.

(b) *Improving standing in consumer markets*: Clearly there is a major problem with the product and how it is perceived by consumers. Bradflax needs repositioning as an attractive, good quality product at an economic price. This calls for modifications to all four marketing mix variables. Guidance about the nature and direction of such modifications can come from an examination of Bradflax's customers at both consumer and retail levels.

Consumers might well be: young couples establishing

a first home and older couples buying to replace worn or outdated carpet. Although it is likely that buyers are heavily motivated by low cost, they will still expect attractive design and good quality. Further, they are not necessarily all from the lower socio-economic grades. Bradflax might be marketed to ABC_1s as a smart product at a sensible price. As carpet purchases are infrequent, consumers are almost certain not to have expertise in carpet buying and will seek information from sources such as advertising, salesmen and friends.

Retail buyers seeking products that, by a combination of turnover and margin, are profitable to sell and which will enhance the image and attractiveness of their shops.

Product – a new range of shades and patterns, tested on samples of the target market, should be developed and, if technically feasible, the products rough texture and shedding problems should be improved.

Price – this should be competitive with other flax carpets and significantly lower than traditional carpets.

Promotion – advertising in mass media – television or national press – is not appropriate. The company does not have the necessary financial resources and in any case, as there are so few carpet purchasers at any one time, mass media would be absurdly expensive in cost-per-thousand terms. The company could consider advertising in specialist media for home furnishing and decorating and the use of in-store display. The advertising and promotional material should emphasise Bradflax's quality, range of patterns and textures. As discussed next, good distribution is essential, and the company should review the effectiveness of its sales force.

Distribution – this is of great importance in the purchase decision process for consumer durables, and it is essential to obtain good stock levels, display and support from retail sales personnel. It is just as important for retailers to be re-educated about the improved Bradflax as it is for consumers. The company should promote the new product to the trade and ensure that the margins and sales incentives are sufficient to obtain prominent display for the product and promotional material and to encourage sales personnel to offer Bradflax to consumers with confidence and enthusiasm.

Audit and review – the company must establish a procedure for assessing the achievement of its marketing objectives and instituting modifications as they become necessary.

(c) *Entering industrial markets*: Whilst the principles of industrial marketing are very similar to those of consumer marketing, there are differences of emphasis and application, and it might be necessary to appoint specialist personnel. The success of Bradflax in industrial markets will depend on how well it meets buyers' criteria such as price, durability, ease of fitting, delivery and flame proofing. By identifying these factors and making assessments of size, stability and growth of demand, the company can decide which markets, if any, to enter. It will then be necessary to follow much the same procedure as for the consumer market, deciding a market position and designing the marketing mix required.

Obviously, the mix will rely less on promotion, although literature and specification sheets will be required. As success will depend greatly on the ability of the salesforce to locate and influence the personnel who determine purchase, some extra training or recruitment might be necessary.

Product designs should be more restrained than for the consumer market and price will be subject to much closer examination by buyers. Again, it is essential to monitor and review progress.

(d) *New Product Development*: As stated above, this can be costly and involve high risk. However, it might be possible to do some low-cost development of products, such as table mats or floor mats, where existing processes and distribution can be used. For the future, the company could consider expanding into conventional carpets and the more general fabric furnishing market. However, this is a more strategic level of decision and it is first necessary to develop and so consolidate, as far as is possible, the company's existing area of activity.

(e) *Summary*: The company's sales revenue appears to provide the basis for a return to profitability to be achieved by, where appropriate, cost reductions and the regaining of sales volume.

The strategy for sales increase in the short term should be:

- a relaunch of Bradflax in the consumer market
- a move into selected industrial markets.

In the longer term:

- a move into more industrial markets
- the development of new products.

Appendix 2

Preparing for Marketing Examinations
1. Understanding the subject.
2. Communicating your answer.
3. Preparing for marketing examinations.
4. Organising your study.

Understanding the Subject by Relating it to 'Real-World' Marketing

Success in any subject depends not only on ability and hard work but also on efficient use of time. This requires systematic and sustained study – one hour's concentrated study can be more effective than an evening's browsing through a textbook.

The study of marketing has particular requirements and characteristics ensuing from the nature of the subject. Marketing is a practical subject concerned with the analysis and solution of business problems, and this is more and more a feature of examination and coursework questions. Such questions require students to demonstrate their understanding of the subject by applying their knowledge, rather than simply repeating it.

In your study, therefore, it is essential to reflect on how the subject occurs in the business world – how companies use (or do *not* use) the principles contained in the textbooks. Marketing is a subject that affects you every day – you experience marketing at home, at the shops, at work and at college. So, when you see advertisements on television or in the paper or choose products, consider the connection between your observations and experience and what you have studied.

Communicate Your Answer

Students often feel uncertain about the answers required by marketing questions. Here are suggestions that can assist in overcoming this problem.

(a) *Structure*: Answers in any subject must have a structure – therefore plan this before beginning to write the answer. Note down the points you intend to use and then structure them into a logical framework. Very simply, this structure should have a *beginning* or introduction, where the problem and subject are stated and the scope of the answer outlined; a *middle*, which contains the bulk of the answer, examining and explaining the question; and an *end*, where conclusions can be drawn, recommendations made and a summary given.

   Some questions, for example numbers 5, 24 and 50 in the text, require the application of marketing knowledge and theory to a particular problem. One way to answer such a question is to go through the problem, applying relevant parts of the theory separately to each part of the problem. While this method can be successful, it is much simpler (and safer) to give an introduction to the question and an outline to the theory in the first part of the answer and in the second part to apply this theory to the problem given and make any necessary conclusions, recommendations and summary.

   Another type of question, for example numbers 1, 15 and 43, requires an explanation of a particular topic. In such cases, the structure of the answer should be developed from the terms given in the title.

(b) *Examples*: Irrespective of the type of question, the objective is for the student to demonstrate understanding of the subject. With a problem-type question this is achieved by relating relevant knowledge to the problem. For questions of the topic-type, the student can show that he understands the subject (rather than is simply reciting it) by the use of examples.

   It will be remembered how examples given in lectures illustrate a topic. In the same way they indicate comprehension in 'written answers.

(c) *Originality*: Many students are concerned about being original or using 'their own ideas'. The advice here is much the same as for the use of examples. Your own observations and conclusions can illuminate an answer and indicate to the examiner that you understand the topic and have given it some thought. It is quite possible that your ideas will be the basis of a new approach to the topic in the future, but at the examination stage of your career it is probably more appropriate to incorporate your thoughts within the main body of a more conventional answer to the question.

(d) *Brevity*: Over-long answers are almost certain to lose marks. They become boring and tiring for the examiner to read and leave you less time to answer other questions. The solution is not merely to write answers that are short but to write answers that are relevant. Read the question carefully, make a plan and ensure that you are not verbose, repeat points nor introduce extraneous material.

Terms used in or central to the question should be defined and explained, not only to show understanding but also to assist in explanation of the question. However, it is acceptable to refer to further relevant terms without explanation.

(e) *Layout*: Remember that marketing is a business subject where conventional essays of the type used in subjects such as History and English might not be appropriate. Develop a report style of presentation using numbered sections, subheadings and short paragraphs. Points should be listed and indented to stand out. Do not be reluctant to leave large areas of the page unwritten.

All this will enhance the conceptual structure of your answer and make it easier for the examiner to read.

Preparing for Marketing Examinations

Preparation for an examination begins at the start of a course and you should obtain a syllabus in order to ascertain its scope. You will find that study is much more difficult if you do not have constant access to the necessary books. Therefore, buy all the *basic reading* textbooks recommended, often only one. Textbooks can appear expensive, but in fact they are a very good investment in the context of the amount of time you spend studying and the career prospects that are opened up by examination success. Thoroughly investigate the conditions of the examination; the number of papers, their duration, compulsory questions, the number of questions to be answered and the number of marks for each question or section. With case studies (see Appendix 1), find out whether the case is available before the examination day and if so how long before.

If you have organised your studies efficiently, you should begin your final revision period for the examination with a concise set of notes covering the syllabus. The next task is to identify key areas of the course which will form the basis for examination questions. These areas and the emphasis vary but the following topics appear fairly consistently.

(a) Definition and functions of Marketing, the marketing concept, consumer orientation, differential advantage, the marketing mix.

(b) Marketing's role in the company, relationship with other company functions, role in deciding and achieving corporate objectives.

(c) Marketing Planning, Strategy and Forecasting, the marketing plan and setting marketing objectives, determination of the level and mix of marketing expenditure, diversification and growth strategies, sales forecasting.

(d) Marketing organisation, the brand/product and market manager systems.

(e) Consumer Behaviour, consumer behaviour theory, models of consumer behaviour, attitudes and attitude measurement, reference groups, lifestyle, diffusion and adoption.

(f) Market segmentation, demographics, socio-economic, ACORN, SAGACITY.

(g) Market Research, research design, random and quota sampling, questionnaire design, primary and secondary sources of data, desk research, *ad hoc* research, continuous research and panels, retail audits and consumer panels, qualitative and quantitative research, omnibus surveys, test marketing, observation studies, advertising research, copy and media research, clinical research.

(h) Product and product development, product life cycle, strategies throughout the cycle, product positioning and branding, product mix.

(i) Marketing Communications, Advertising and Promotion, the communication process and models, advertising objectives, campaign planning, organisation of the UK advertising industry, agencies, the promotional mix, setting the advertising budget, media planning, sales promotion, publicity and public relations.

(j) Pricing, price and psychology, price-setting for new products.

(k) Distribution, the UK distribution structure and the forces for change, physical distribution management.

(l) Sales management, sales force size, sales force territory design, payment methods.

(m) Industrial Marketing, the organisational buying decision, comparison between consumer and industrial buying.

(n) International Marketing, comparison between national and international marketing, multinational trading, exporting, franchising and local manufacture, entering overseas markets.

(o) The Marketing of Services, types of service market, comparison between product and service marketing.

(p) Marketing for non-profit objectives, comparison with marketing for profit.

(q) Consumerism, the nature and rise of consumerism in the UK, consumerism and marketing management, the economics of advertising.

(r) Consumer Protection in the UK, the significance of consumer protection for marketing management.

Obtain past examination papers and use these in conjunction with this book to give a rough indication of what to expect in an examination. Practice answering questions under time constraints continually during the course, and compare your answer with the model answer, if necessary rewriting incorrect passages. Make a point of learning from previous errors or omissions.

In the days before the examination do not resort to cramming, which is usually a last despairing effort to learn material which should have been covered months ago. Burning the midnight oil only leaves you mentally and physically fatigued. Aim to arrange your revision and non-academic affairs so that you are mentally alert and physically fit as you enter the examination room, *not* tired and haggard. Give yourself plenty of time to reach the room where the examination is to be held and make sure you have all the necessary equipment: ruler, pen, pencil, eraser, etc.

Read through the paper thoroughly and construct a rough timetable, e.g. if you are asked to answer five questions in three hours you should spend 30–35 minutes per question, allowing approximately 10 minutes initial reading of the paper and 10 minutes final reading through your answers.

If you have a choice of questions, then during your preliminary reading of the paper you should indicate which questions you feel competent to answer. Make a final choice of questions to be answered, picking those questions from your list of 'possibles' that you feel most confident about. Your best questions should be attempted first. Make sure you understand every part of the question and what is required from you before attempting an answer.

Your answers should be planned and written following the points recommended in Section 2. Present your answers clearly and legibly; research shows that good handwriting and clear presentation increase marks. If you succeed in meeting your time constraints you should have time at the end of the examination to reread your answers, making any corrections or minor improvements that are necessary.

Organising Your Study

A common obstacle to success is the lack of a plan of study. Such a plan is essential in order to cover the syllabus properly. A rigid timetable is not usually a good idea, but you must set yourself a certain feasible number of hours study time a week. Get an overall view of the workload by assessing how long each section of the syllabus will take you to cover. Then, at the beginning of each week, you can construct a timetable for that week. Ensure that your plan of studies allows six to eight weeks for revision, prior to the examination.

During each weekly section of your work plan set yourself time constraints for completing certain pieces of work. Practice at working under time pressure will be of considerable benefit during the examination. Set aside certain times for study, as habit and routine are important foundations for keeping to the plan. When studying, observe the following points.

(a) Concentrate your attention by eliminating all sources of distraction.

(b) Start work immediately you sit down – do not wait for inspiration, as it rarely comes!

(c) Set yourself a reasonable task or set of tasks to complete and work towards achieving this rather than towards simply working until a certain time.

(d) Try to obtain as much information as you can about your progress, by discussing your assignments and essays with your tutor.